THE CYCLOPES

AEOLUS

THRINACIA

The Lestrygonians

CIRCE

Scylla

THE SIRENS

HADES

THE ART
OF
THE ODYSSEY

Howard W. Clarke

PAPERBACKS

This impression 2004
This edition published in 1989 by
arrangement with Prentice-Hall, Inc., by
Bristol Classical Press
an imprint of
Gerald Duckworth & Co. Ltd.
90-93 Cowcross Street, London EC1M 6BF
Tel: 020 7490 7300
Fax: 020 7490 0080
inquiries@duckworth-publishers.co.uk
www.ducknet.co.uk

First published in 1967 by Prentice-Hall, Inc.
© 1967, 1989 by Howard C. Clarke

A catalogue record for this book is available
from the British Library

ISBN 1 85399 052 3

Printed and bound in Great Britain by
Antony Rowe Ltd, Eastbourne

⁓§ CONTENTS §⁓

⋅❧ INTRODUCTION ❧⋅

In 272 B.C. a Greek named Andronicus was captured in a battle in southern Italy and brought as a slave to Rome, where he came to be employed as a schoolmaster. Finding no suitable text for the enlightenment of his young charges, he translated Homer's *Odyssey* into Latin verse around 240 B.C., thus establishing Homeric poetry as the first achievement of Latin literature as it was of Greek. Since then Homeric epic—the *Odyssey* in particular—has retained a primacy of various sorts, as the first and probably the finest example of its genre, the beginning of the Western literary tradition, and the ideal introduction to literature, so simple and so profound, so obvious and so mysterious, so accessible and so elusive, but withal so available to everyone despite limitations of age, culture, or literary awareness. The *Iliad*, like its hero, can be difficult, austere, desperate, but the *Odyssey*, as Livius Andronicus realized when he faced the stolid sons of his Roman masters, is for everyone. The same may be said of this book. It is intended for that overworked abstraction, the general reader (who has to read so many books!), and its aim is to comment on the *Odyssey* in such a way as to increase the pleasure and understanding of a reader either first coming or returning to Homer's great epic. Although this study follows, more or less, the sequence of action in the poem, it is not, except incidentally, a retelling of the story, for as Odysseus himself says at the end of Book XII (452-53), "It goes against the grain with me to repeat a tale already plainly told." [1] Noted in passing, too, are some of the long-standing puzzles of the *Odyssey*'s composition, but they are not solved; instead the emphasis in the present study is to elucidate (and celebrate) What There Is rather than to speculate on What Might Have Been. This tactic is less a maneuver than a dodge, because many of the problems of logic and consistency that began to bedevil scholars in the nineteenth century are still outstanding and though some have ceased to matter much they can still cast their special pall over even the most self-consciously literary criticism. Finally, though this present work presumes to be a literary study, it presupposes no great knowledge of literature, either Greek or general, though it does offer occasional references to other works—particularly, and unavoidably, the *Iliad*—where themes and incidents similar to those in the *Odyssey* are represented. One of the special pleasures of reading Homeric poetry is to see forming there the artistic techniques and concerns that have become characteristic of our whole literary culture; to see them recur in later literature, even when there can be no direct influence, helps to impress us with the sophistication of Homer as an artist and to dissuade us from the hearty Philistinism that views the *Odyssey* as no more than a rattling good collection of sailors' yarns.

This study, then, is an essay in literary explication. Now in Greek epic it is very difficult to separate such explication from linguistic and historical criticism, particularly after the momentous discoveries of the past few years. Thanks to Milman Parry and Albert Lord we know a great deal about the techniques of oral poetry; with a high degree of likelihood we can describe how Homer must have composed his poems and we can appreciate the special qualities and hazards entailed by oral composition.[2] Thanks to Michael Ventris and John Chadwick we can now read much of Linear B, the script used by the Mycenaeans of the Bronze Age (roughly 2000-1000 B.C.) to keep the records of their ramified activities.[3] And thanks to the continuing labors of archaeologists of many different countries, each year adds to the supply of information about the Bronze Age civilization that is the setting of the Homeric poems.[4] Paradoxically, however, much of this information, valuable in itself and for the light it casts on these otherwise obscure centuries, is negative in its application to Homer. Theories of oral composition that are based in part on the practices of contemporary Slavic singers can show how oral poems are composed, but they are less useful in separating good oral poems from bad or in explaining the special fascination of certain oral poems, such as the *Iliad* and the *Odyssey*. The records of the Bronze Age preserved in the Linear B syllabary reveal a palace society—or bureaucracy—remarkable for the industry of its members, the complexity of its operations, and the orderliness of its records, but even after duly acknowledging the spiritual distance between bookkeepers and poets, one can hardly feel that the decipherment of Linear B has brought us closer to the society depicted in Homer's poems. Finally, the archaeologists' findings are plenteous indeed, but at Troy VII A, Homer's Troy, they have been very meager, and, in general, as the physical record of mainland Greece during the Bronze Age becomes more intelligible and more cohesive, the Homeric record seems increasingly discontinuous and heterogeneous.[5] In fact, it is almost a trend now among scholars to stress the gap between Homer and history, and the author of a recent book on Bronze Age Greece has even declined to use Homer's poetry as evidence for the Mycenaean civilization he so selectively described.[6] We have come a long way from the time when Heinrich Schliemann, the first systematic excavator of Bronze Age sites, based his probes on a burning faith that Homeric poetry was a faithful transcript of history. Perhaps now it is best to begin by recalling that the materials of the Homeric poems are myths and the history that finds its way into myths is usually attenuated and idealized, the projection of a people's fantasies, not the record of their activities. Properly understood, the *Aeneid* is also an "historical" poem, and the story of Aeneas' mission that Virgil tells is a mythic rendering of Augustan history—that is, a rendering of history freed from the literalness of the chronicle. It may happen that the *Iliad* and the *Odyssey* will someday seem to have the same relationship to their time that the *Aeneid* has to Augustan Rome—a great poet's descant on the spirit of his age. So the *Iliad* and to a lesser extent the *Odyssey* may use elements of twelfth century (or even sixteenth century) history to localize their plots, but it is a history filtered and refined, a history that subserves the myth of one man whose honor was slighted and whose friend was killed and of another man whose home was despoiled and whose family was imperiled. These myths are the stories of the poems, and it is the second of these stories that will be the subject of this essay.

Of course, to write about Homeric poetry is always presumptuous, for not only are the unknowns many and extensive, but the scholarly record is itself so long that research waits endlessly upon bibliography and the original works subside beneath their vast critical commentaries. The Homeric commentator is in a particularly desperate situation as he confronts this flood of books and articles, for, like it or not, there is little he can say that has not in some form or other been said by his predecessors, who are also—at least by virtue of their getting there first—his betters. Originality in these matters, then, is an illusion, but a benign illusion, and in trying to say a few new things about the *Odyssey* this essay will pay the price—and win the profit—of repeating very many old things. One old thing excepted: the Homeric Question. There is nothing argued in this essay about the problem of authorship that has so long exercised the wits of the learned and the not so learned; instead it will be assumed here that there was a Homer and that in the late eighth century he did write the *Iliad* as we now have it and (then) the *Odyssey*, too, for better or for worse. There are arguments for and against this view (which might be called Sentimental Unitarianism), but none of them much affects what will be said in these pages.

Wherever else I am indebted to other critics for information or insights outside the body of common knowledge, sources are acknowledged in footnotes; and in an appendix are listed some of the more accessible books on Homer and the *Odyssey*. To avoid the inconvenience of page flipping, cited material is wherever possible embodied in the text, and so the footnotes grouped in the rear of the book usually contain only the references themselves.

My acknowledgments cannot be limited to footnotes. Fifteen years ago I attended classes at Harvard where I heard Professors John Finley and Cedric Whitman talk about the *Odyssey*. I am grateful to them for the stimulation of their lectures and for the generosity of their direction some years later of my dissertation on the *Odyssey*. Neither one is responsible for what I have occasionally done with—and to—their views, but much of whatever is good in the following pages must be attributed to their inspiration. I am also grateful to the editors of *The Classical Journal*, the *American Journal of Philology*, and *Indiana Slavic Studies* for permission to re-use material that first appeared in their journals. Finally, I must thank Marian Wilson, typist, critic, and friend.

Introduction to Second Edition, 1989

I am grateful to Peter Jones for suggesting that this book be reprinted, and to John Betts and the Bristol Classical Press for taking up the suggestion. While the text has remained unchanged (apart from the removal of minor *errata*), the endnotes and appendix on further reading have been revised to account for recent and relevant scholarship.

ᵃ§ I §ᵃ

BOOK ONE:

SOME FIRST IMPRESSIONS

I

The hero of the tale which I beg the Muse to help me tell is that resourceful man who roamed the wide world after he had sacked the holy citadel of Troy. He saw the cities of many peoples and he learnt their ways. He suffered many hardships on the high seas in his struggles to preserve his life and bring his comrades home. But he failed to save those comrades, in spite of all his efforts. It was their own sin that brought them to their doom, for in their folly they devoured the oxen of Hyperion the Sun, and the god saw to it that they should never return. This is the tale I pray the divine Muse to unfold to us. Begin it, goddess, at whatever point you will. (I, 1-10)

One of the first impressions one has on leafing through the *Odyssey* is that its hero does not appear until Book V where Homer begins with his homecoming adventures. Odysseus' personal story is preceded by the story of his son Telemachus. This story, the so-called *Telemacheia,* is in turn preceded by the Council of the Gods at the beginning of Book I, which itself is preceded by the induction or proem. These ten introductory lines (quoted above) are the poet's traditional invocation of the Muse to assist him as he tells his song, and they are often spaced apart from the rest of Book I, as well they might be, since much of what they tell us is not what the poem tells us, and conversely there are important elements of the poem, such as the Suitors, that are not registered in the proem. First of all, Odysseus, "that resourceful man who roamed the wide world" (1-2), is not a roamer out to see the world. Later writers—Tennyson is a familiar example ("I cannot rest from travel; I will drink/Life to the lees") and Dante a more illustrious one—could make of Odysseus a vagabond and a quester, the incarnation of restlessness, enterprise, and curiosity. But Homer's Odysseus has a goal—his home in Ithaca and his family, Penelope and Telemachus. However often he must interrupt his journey, the goal is always there.

5

For most readers, the glory of the *Odyssey* is precisely these inter-
ruptions, and so it may seem strange that Homer mentions none of
the better-known adventures here, nor does he speak of the troubles
in Ithaca that will occupy Odysseus throughout the whole second
half of the poem. Instead he speaks, oddly, of how Odysseus visited
many cities and learned the ways of their inhabitants. This is not
so. About the only "city" that Odysseus visits is that of the Phae-
acians, and there he finds that their ways are not much different
from the ways of most Greeks in the Bronze Age. So, in point of fact,
this is not a very accurate or systematic introduction to the poem,
although there is no reason why a proem should have to serve as a
table of contents. But whatever this proem may leave out, it does
make two other points that the attentive reader should notice, one
less obvious than the other. First, it gives an importance to Odysseus'
comrades that will later be obscured by the poem and overlooked
by most readers. It is difficult to think very long or very hard about
Odysseus' comrades. Apart from the nervous Eurylochus who leads
the first reconnaissance party to Circe's house in Book X, escapes
back to Odysseus and then refuses to guide him back, and the silly
young Elpenor who gets drunk at the end of Book X and falls off
Circe's roof, they are, for the most part, a nameless and faceless
crew. But though Odysseus is often at odds with his men, his worst
suffering on his troubled voyage was experienced, as he tells the
Phaeacians, when so many of the men were caught by Scylla in
Book XII and held out their hands to him as they were fed into
Scylla's six monstrous mouths; and it was characteristic of Odysseus
that when they camped on Circe's island it was he himself who let
the hungry men sleep while he headed inland, killed a stag, and
carried it back for a day-long banquet (X, 144-188). This is Odysseus
the leader, who, as the introduction stresses, wanted to save his com-
rades and bring them home. Odysseus the protector of anonymous
sailors in the first half of the poem becomes King Odysseus in the
second half, the head of a family and the leader of a state. Hence
the introduction, after describing the familiar Odysseus, the traveler
and visitor, goes on to emphasize the less familiar responsibilities of
Odysseus, his accountability to his followers. The proem's intro-
duction of Odysseus in his double role reminds us that there are,
in fact, two levels of action in the poem, the personal and the
social. On the former level, the *Odyssey* is the story of one man's re-
turn to his home and his family; on the latter level, of the king who
returns to his native land, drives out the usurpers, and reestab-
lishes his rule in justice and prosperity.

The second point the introduction now stresses is the reason for the destruction of Odysseus' sailors. They perished, we read, because of their folly, their "sin." It is good to know this, for otherwise it would appear that Odysseus failed his men, and the captain who cannot look after his crew would hardly make a responsible and compassionate king. But Homer emphasizes that their death was a punishment for their own wrongdoing, despite Odysseus' best efforts. They did wrong and they were punished. This is not just an isolated incident, for this is what will happen throughout the *Odyssey:* the good will be rewarded and the bad will be punished. This is, generally, a very moral poem in which the gods are operating to guarantee the moral order, and Odysseus will appear at the end as their viceroy and their scourge, Zeus' Angry Man. It is morally a very tidy and reassuring poem, and for all its witches and monsters the world of the *Odyssey* is somehow a more comfortable world than the comparatively nihilistic vacuum of the *Iliad* where passions overwhelm principles, where capricious gods rule by divine spite, and where Achilles in loneliness and uncertainty suffers to create an order of personal dignity. There are no Hectors, guiltless and noble, who must die in the *Odyssey*—only disobedient sailors and destructive Suitors. This is not the place to speculate whether this represents an advance in the moral awareness of Western man or a clarification of the developing Greek concept of justice, or even if this represents the view of a Homer grown old, who, after the heat of the *Iliad* in which Achilles suffered injustice and innocent soldiers perished amid the inequities of warfare, now looks at life anew and accepts the gods' dispositions and the world's judgments. All of this has been urged in consequence of these lines from the proem and with good reason, though one should be cautious about attributing abstract and weighty ideologies to Homer or discovering beneficent moral purposes in the activities of the gods. It seems to be a fact of Homeric epic that the divine characters follow and reflect the human in their attitudes and actions. The *Iliad* is a story of injustice among powerful men and the gods of the *Iliad* are likewise powerful and arbitrary; the *Odyssey* is a success story, an account of how a good hero defeats evil men, and so we should not be surprised that the gods of the *Odyssey* seem interested in making justice triumph. The *Iliad,* in its concluding action, pits Achilles against Hector, a good man against another good man, whereas in the *Odyssey* there is no doubt that the Suitors are very bad indeed and will suffer punishment at the hands of a man who is in every way their superior.[1] Of course, the question is still open as to what poetic or spiritual impulse led Homer from the story of Achilles to the story of Odysseus, but for now it is enough to note, after the *Iliad*, the altered atmosphere of this poem. The *Odyssey* is a very worldly poem and it celebrates the world's morality of just deserts.

II

Yet all the gods were sorry for him, except Poseidon, who pursued the heroic Odysseus with relentless malice till the day when he reached his own country. (I, 19-21)

The introduction ends with the poet's request to the Muse to begin at whatever point she chooses. The point she chooses is a Council of the Gods, where the Olympian divinities meet to hear Athena's sorrow over the fate of Odysseus. Notably absent is Poseidon, who is angry with Odysseus for having blinded his son Polyphemus, the Cyclops. It is altogether appropriate that this god of the sea, as sullen and dangerous as his element, should harass Odysseus, himself so eminent a representative of civilized values. This conflict between Poseidon and Odysseus is reflected in and symbolized by the geography of the poem, for practically all of Odysseus' journey is over water, and many of the main scenes of the *Odyssey* take place on islands. In fact, Odysseus does better on islands than on the mainland where he has short, costly encounters with the Cicones, the Laestrygonians, and the Cyclops Polyphemus. Even including the island of Thrinacia, where his men eat the Cattle of the Sun, the islands in the poem offer Odysseus a measure of relief along with their indigenous dangers. The rich and luxuriant island opposite the Cyclops' home provides his men refuge while Odysseus is dealing with Polyphemus; on the floating island of Aeolia Odysseus is entertained for a month and receives the bag of winds; Odysseus and his men spend a year on Circe's island Aeaea; Odysseus hears the beautiful song of the Sirens from their island; and finally, after drifting for days after his boat is destroyed, Odysseus lands on Calypso's island Ogygia where he spends seven years. More important than any of these, however, is Scherie, the island home of the Phaeacians, that for Odysseus, hard pressed by storm and shipwreck after he leaves Calypso, will represent a temporary salvation. But Scherie is but a stage in his journey to his final goal, the island of Ithaca, the climax of the poem's series of islands in that Odysseus in Ithaca will not only be the saved but also the savior. In each instance, but particularly in Scherie, the island is a symbol of security in an angry and arbitrary world. For Odysseus it is the dry land of rescue after persecution by the sea god Poseidon, a stable point in his uncertain and dismaying progress.

The barbarism and vagueness of the sea is particularly applicable to the social significance of the *Odyssey*. For the sea is primal violence ever encroaching upon the gains of civilization. Poseidon's persecution of Odysseus was invoked by a curse and animated by a desire for vengeance; his weapons are storm and wave. The curse and the vendetta are the moral sanctions of the most primitive society; against them the poem counterpoises the boat, the island, and the ideal of justice, in an ascending scale of civilized values— the boat, be it raft or ship, by which Odysseus makes his way across Poseidon's sea, the island, like Scherie or Ithaca, in which men live together and nature is benign, and the justice as it is done to the good and the bad that is one of the moral themes of the poem. Far from being just another of Odysseus' trials, the sea (always distrusted, sometimes hated, by the Greeks) becomes an almost archetypal image of undifferentiated nature which must be endured by man and overcome by his efforts. The power of the sea is super-human and its effect is dehumanizing, robbing man of his friends and possessions and threatening to rob him of his very life. For it is the sea that reduces Odysseus from Achaean hero to Lear's "unaccommodated man . . . a poor, bare, forked animal," stripping him first of his crew before it casts him onto the shore of Calypso's island and then even of his clothes when he swims ashore onto the island of the Phaeacians.[2] And were Odysseus to drown he would die an unheroic death altogether abhorrent to the Greeks, with no survivors to testify to the glory of his going and with no tomb to mark his final resting place.[3]

With sea and land so meaningfully balanced in the *Odyssey*, it is very appropriate that this symbolic scheme should be grounded in a simile at the end of the poem where Odysseus' return to Penelope is described as being as sweet to her as the sight of land to shipwrecked sailors who manage at last to struggle onto the solid earth (XXIII, 233-38). This simile neatly preserves the contrast between the other islands and Ithaca and between the first and second halves of the poem. In his travels Odysseus was the shipwrecked sailor struggling toward land; now in Ithaca, triumphant over the Suitors and reunited with Penelope, he has become the solid earth of stability, the incarnation of victory over disordering nature and the guarantor of personal security and social prosperity.

III

Poseidon, however, was now gone on a visit to the distant Ethiopians. (I, 22)

Poseidon is absent when this Council of the Gods convenes, gone, characteristically, to "the farthest outposts of mankind" (I, 23). In the absence of Poseidon Athena feels she can make an appeal for Odysseus. Absence, whether voluntary or enforced, is important in Homer because power is dependent on presence and cannot be deployed from a distance. Odysseus can be helped here because Poseidon is not around, just as in the *Iliad* the Achaeans could be helped once Hera had lured Zeus off to Mount Ida. Indeed, a point to be considered later is that both epics are about absent heroes, Achilles in his tent and Odysseus on his travels, and both at Troy and at Ithaca things go very badly while they are away.

IV

Meanwhile the rest of the gods had assembled in the palace of Olympian Zeus, and the Father of men and gods opened a discussion among them. He had been thinking of that nobleman, Aegisthus, whom Agamemnon's son Orestes killed, to his own great renown. (I, 26-30)

Zeus begins the deliberations of the gods by mentioning the story of Agamemnon's unhappy return home from the Trojan War. This is a story that will often be heard in the *Odyssey* and should be understood at the beginning. While Agamemnon was away at war, his wife Clytemnestra was seduced by Aegisthus, who then joined with her to assassinate Agamemnon on his return. Both Aegisthus and Clytemnestra were later put to death by the royal children Orestes and Electra (who is not mentioned in the *Odyssey*). This story, repeated too often in the poem to be regarded as incidental illustration, operates as a kind of leitmotif. Its relevance is of course obvious: Clytemnestra = Penelope, Orestes = Telemachus, Agamemnon = Odysseus. The story is a warning to Odysseus, an inspiration for Telemachus, and a vindication of Penelope. Its first appearance is here at the very beginning of the poem where, like a phrase in an overture, it can be fixed in the reader's mind, and it will reappear frequently throughout the poem, at length in Books III, IV, XI, and XXIV. In each retelling significant details relate this story to the action of the *Odyssey*. When recounted here by Zeus it illustrates the goodness and justice of the gods and man's responsibility for his own rash conduct, both main themes of the poem and both appropriately sounded in the palace of Zeus before activities commence at the human level.

When Telemachus first hears part of the story from Athena in Book I (298-300), the stress is on the example of Orestes, whereas in Books III (255-75 and 303-10) and IV (524-40), after we have seen the Suitors in action in Odysseus' house, the emphasis shifts to the dastardliness of Aegisthus. In Book IV the twenty-man ambush set by Aegisthus suggests the twenty-man ambush to be staged by the Suitors in their attempt to capture and kill Telemachus, the comparison of the slain Agamemnon to an ox felled at its manger reminds us of the many oxen slaughtered by the Suitors, the wholesale slaughter of 535-36 prefigures the mass slaying of the Suitors in Book XXIII, and the advice given to Menelaus to hurry back to his land warns Telemachus not to dawdle on his journey to Pylos and Sparta. Next, the longer account by Agamemnon himself in Book XI mentions Clytemnestra, and although Agamemnon assures Odysseus that Penelope is not that kind of a girl, still the example is not wholly lost on Odysseus. In his eagerness to magnify the cruelty of his wife, Agamemnon reveals that "the most pitiable thing of all was the cry I heard from Cassandra, daughter of Priam, whom that foul traitress Clytemnestra murdered at my side" (421-23). It is odd that Agamemnon mentions Cassandra, whom he was bringing back as a concubine from Troy, since his liaison with her was used by Clytemnestra to justify her part in his assassination. Homer otherwise avoids mention of Cassandra, just as he avoids mention of such other extenuating circumstances as the curse on the House of Atreus (Atreus was Agamemnon's father), Aegisthus' justification for seeking vengeance (his father Thyestes was tricked by Atreus into eating his own children), and Orestes' matricide (on the orders of Apollo he killed Clytemnestra). Homer wants to keep his example clear and the issues simple, so he has chosen those details of the Agamemnon myth that will best serve the story of Odysseus.

One small change he has made that is very important for the *Odyssey* is his vivid description of Agamemnon and his men being cut down amidst the laden banquet tables, their blood mingling with the wine set out for the feast. It will also be at a feast that Odysseus will finish off the Suitors. So here we have the perfect picture of the desecrated feast, the banquet of hospitality and welcome turned to carnage. Considering that Aegisthus has chosen to violate what throughout the *Odyssey* is symbolic of peace and communion (see below, p. 15), we can appreciate the great effectiveness of Homer's using this version of the myth rather than the version

more familiar to us from Aeschylus' *Agamemnon,* in which Aga-
memnon is killed in the bath. Even Homer's words suggest the
Suitors: "And all around me my companions were cut down in
ruthless succession, like white-tusked swine slaughtered in the man-
sion of some great and wealthy lord, for a wedding, a club-banquet,
or a sumptuous public feast" (XI, 412-15). This echoes Athena's
questions about the Suitors' partying in I, 226: "Is this a public
feast or a wedding? Or a club-banquet?" Finally, Agamemnon's
brief mention of Clytemnestra in Book XXIV, completes the Aga-
memnon motif. Penelope is praised: her glory will be made a song
by the gods themselves. For Clytemnestra, on the contrary, "her
name will be cursed wherever she is sung" (221). Here at last the
fury has abated and the violence of the past will become the songs
of the future. The cruelty of Clytemnestra and the loyalty of Pe-
nelope will soon be only what the storytellers can make of them.

This use of the Agamemnon motif has a powerful effectiveness
in the *Odyssey.* It sharpens the two great themes of the poem, love
and justice, by presenting them in what was in Greek mythology
two of their most shameful betrayals, the adultery of Clytemnestra
and the intrigue of Aegisthus. This motif acts as a dramatic
paradigm, multiplying and clarifying meaning, and it tightens the
plot of the *Odyssey,* which inclines to be discursive and episodic.
But most important, it focuses the whole notion of the poem in a
few lines, warning Homer's characters of the precedents of recent
history and reminding Homer's readers of the meaning of the
Odyssey.

V

What a lamentable thing it is that men should blame the gods and
regard us as the source of their troubles, when it is their own wicked-
ness that brings them sufferings worse than any which Destiny allots
them. (I, 32-34)

Zeus now makes his opening statement in which he distinguishes
between the gods' responsibility for men, which he suggests is
benign and protective, and man's responsibility for himself and
for the consequences of his acts. The Zeus of the *Odyssey,* who can
indulge here in theological speculations, is, as we have seen, quite
different from the Zeus of the *Iliad,* reluctantly involved in the
partisan politics of warfare. This may represent a step in the evolu-
tion from power to goodness within the Greek concept of divinity,
a process many critics find dramatized in Aeschylus' *Prometheus*

Bound, or it may—more likely—be accounted for by the differences in plot, character, and setting between the two epics. But here Zeus claims that the gods do try to warn men against wrongdoing, and at the end of the poem it is Zeus who urges that peace with justice be established in Ithaca.

Also, unlike the situation in the *Iliad,* one divinity dominates the action of the *Odyssey.* The difference between the two epics in this respect is probably less theological than poetic. Homeric religion tends to reflect the human world, and the human world of the *Iliad* with its array of warriors, its series of conflicts, and its sympathies divided fairly equally between Achaean and Trojan brought out a corresponding diversity, contentiousness, and involvement of the Olympian world. The action of the *Odyssey,* on the other hand, is so often unreal in its first half and unheroic in its second that it hardly admits of a divine parallel—and no god would be tempted to aid the likes of the Suitors.

The *Odyssey,* as its name implies, is all about one man, Odysseus, and so the divine apparatus is limited to one divinity. This is Athena who here pleads for Odysseus and throughout the poem will constantly protect and guide him, rewarding his fidelity as she dares and helps him to punish the wicked Suitors. One might call her his patron saint, were it not so misleading to introduce Christian notions into discussions of Greek gods. For it is basic to Greek religion that gods as powerful as Zeus and Athena are interested only in powerful men. It may be the consolation of the weak and the afflicted Christian that God loves him and will reward him, but this is not true of the Greeks, whose religion made provision for neither love nor rewards. Zeus and his fellow gods could not care less about the meek and the mild, but they are irresistibly attracted to the powerful of the earth, to the heroes, the people Homer describes in his poems. Hence Athena protects Odysseus because he has the skill and cleverness and strength that are also her characteristics. In a famous scene in Book XIII, 329-32, Athena must admit to Odysseus: "I cannot desert you in your misfortunes: you are so civilized, so intelligent, so self-possessed." Athena literally cannot resist Odysseus; she *must* help her heroic protégé since the qualities he shares with her give him an option on her services. So often will we be seeing her help him that we must at the outset recognize a paradox of Homeric religion: when a Homeric hero is assisted by a god it is not a sign that he is weak, but rather that he is strong.

Readers of Homer's epics are sometimes disappointed by the extent and the abruptness of the gods' involvement in human affairs (is it really necessary for Athena to appear as a Phaeacian just to mark the length of Odysseus' discus throw at VIII, 193-97?), and they feel cheated—sometimes with good reason—when a god appears at the fateful moment to divert an arrow that is about to land in a hero's ear. But it is well to remember that this is often Homer's way of indicating that a hero thus favored is probably the kind of man who could dodge the arrow anyway, and the presence of the god is a sign of his heroism. The reader of Homer who feels uncomfortable about the gods' interventions will find some consolation if he perceives that the gods generally operate only in power situations. They are invariably absent from the great scenes of the *Odyssey*, like Odysseus' adventures, his meeting with Nausicaa, or his reunion with Penelope. The *Odyssey*, however, does begin with the gods (it ends with them too), just like, for example, many of Euripides' plays, but whereas in Euripides we feel that there is a falling off when the human actors appear, that they are victims in a larger struggle, and that Euripides' song, like that of Frost's Oven Bird, is "what to make of a diminished thing," the heroes of Homer are neither diminished nor debilitated in their struggles for glory; they can rival and even surpass their immortal protectors because they are human and mortal, and because the time is short in which they must "win glory or give it to others" (*Iliad* XII, 328, trans. Lattimore).

VI

The Suitors came swaggering in and took their seats in rows on the settles and chairs. Their squires poured water on their hands and the maids put piles of bread in baskets beside them, while the pages filled the mixing-bowls to the brim with drink. They helped themselves to the good things spread before them; and when all had satisfied their hunger and thirst, the Suitors turned their thoughts to other pleasures, to the music and dancing without which no banquet is complete. (I, 144-52)

Once Athena has made her plea for Odysseus and won the acquiescence of Zeus, she comes down from Olympus to Ithaca to encourage Telemachus and send him on his journey to Pylos and Sparta. In Ithaca her first view of the Suitors is at dinner, and this is our first view of a scene and an action that will pervade the *Odyssey*. The scene is the feast, the action is eating. Everyone eats in the *Odyssey* and everyone (except, perhaps, the Cyclops) offers everyone else something to eat. In fact, at a couple of places characters eat each other. This is perhaps appropriate for the poem of

Odysseus, who in the *Iliad* insisted (XIX, 225), against Achilles, that the Achaeans should be fed before being sent back into battle. But in the *Odyssey* there is so much more—about one in thirty lines concerns the preparation or consumption of food, or hunger, greed, drinking, and so on. These lines should not be overlooked, even though the sameness of detail tempts a reader to skip over the recurrent scenes of feasting. Mention of eating begins in the very opening lines of the prologue where we read that the crime that doomed Odysseus' comrades was that they devoured the Cattle of the Sun. The other great wrong of the poem, the Suitors' conduct toward the absent Odysseus' house and family, is also set in terms of eating when Telemachus tells Athena in Book I (250-51) and Menelaus in Book IV (318), "They are eating me out of house and home." Food is also the Lotus Eaters' weapon against Odysseus and his men, drink is Odysseus' weapon against Polyphemus, and the Cyclopes, Laestrygonians, and Scylla are all cannibals. Odysseus' grimmest wisdom is reserved for hunger, when as a beggar among the Suitors he first tells Eumaeus (XVII, 286-89), "If there is anything that a man can't conceal it is a ravening belly—that utter curse, the cause of so much trouble to mankind, which even prompts them to fit out great ships and sail the barren seas, bringing death and destruction to their enemies." In the same book, after being hit by a stool, he tells Antinous "This blow from Antinous was brought on me by my wretched belly, that cursed thing men have to thank for so much trouble" (473-74).

Usually the feeding in the *Odyssey* proceeds under more normal circumstances than these, and Homer uses his banquets to keynote the whole poem. We have seen (above, p. 11) how Homer's choice of a banquet as the setting for Agamemnon's murder gave that sad story an extra dimension of horror. Homer can also make a banquet dramatize the effects of sin, as when the roast and raw meat groaned on the spits following the slaughter of the Cattle of the Sun in Book XII (395-96). But generally the feast symbolizes social cosmos. "Under primitive conditions every banquet has a sacral significance. Anyone who eats and drinks in the company of men is united with them by a sacred bond; the admission to a meal means the admission into peace and protection." [4] Hospitality is important in Homeric society and Zeus himself is the God of Hospitality. (When Odysseus thinks he has been deceived by his Phaeacian hosts in Book XIII, 209-14, he calls upon "Zeus, the suppliants' god," to punish them.) The banquet is the traditional scene of hospitality and communal good will, and much of the action of the *Odyssey* takes place at banquets of one sort or another.

Similarly, the denial, interruption, or perversion of the banquet can signal chaos, as Shakespeare knew when first Banquo's murderer and then his ghost interrupted Lady Macbeth's banquet and unmanned Macbeth (III, 4), and the banquet that began as a microcosm of Macbeth's kingdom ended "with most admired disorder." [5] All this is applicable to the Suitors, who not only devour Odysseus' goods but also destroy the form and meaning of the banquet by their endless, purposeless, disruptive carousing. Banquets are usually reserved to mark occasions or to celebrate specific events in accepted ways—a homecoming, for instance, or a visit. Two instances in the *Odyssey* are instructive. It was a homecoming feast that Aegisthus arranged to celebrate Agamemnon's return to Mycenae —and it turned into a mass murder (XI, 405-20). Later in the poem we read that Heracles once played host to Iphitus (from whom Odysseus received his famous bow), feasted him—and then killed him (XXI, 22-30). But at least these feasts, however bloody their end, had a reason for being—a statement which is not true of the Suitors' perpetual banquet. Thus Athena in Book I is puzzled by their actions and cannot describe their banqueting: "What is the meaning of this banquet? Who are all these people? And what is your concern in the affair? No sign of a subscription supper here! Perhaps it is a dinner-party or a wedding-feast?" (225-26) Here the very questions stress the utter formlessness and indefinability of the Suitors' barbarous behavior. Their gluttony fits into none of the accepted categories of eating, as its purpose is less the sustenance of the Suitors than the destruction of Odysseus' household. For the purposes of the poem, it is microcosmic of the disorder in Ithaca.

The quality of the Suitors' feasts may be wholly negative, but at least it may be said that they are abundantly supplied; these young louts eat and drink mightily. But even when feasting off another man's food they are grudging of their loot. When Odysseus appears as a hungry beggar in Book XVII he is only given something to eat after being maltreated and insulted by Antinous. (The Suitors are wary; this beggar might just turn out to be a god.) With this hungry stranger among them the Suitors are now given ample opportunity to redouble their guilt, and one of their number, conscious of this, even reproves Antinous for having thrown a stool at Odysseus. The presence of Odysseus the beggar at the banqueting in these later books of the poem is most significant. The irony of King Odysseus disguised as a poor old man and being abused by his wife's wooers is obvious enough, but on the symbolic level Odysseus's constant and pesky interruptions of the Suitors' feasting strips their banquet of the last shred of harmony that normally dignifies communal feeding.

Odysseus is giving the Suitors a taste of their own appalling behavior. At times one is even tempted to sympathize with the Suitors: Odysseus *is* making a pest of himself and he should, one feels, be a little less relentless. But a reaction like this is a measure of Homer's success in showing how Odysseus irritates the Suitors and exposes the inhospitableness of those who are abusing the hospitality of Odysseus' family. Odysseus is wrecking their banquet just as they have wrecked the principle of the banquet, and he is fortifying himself with the wrath he will expend at the poem's final banquet of blood. The Suitors, then, steal food as well as waste it (XIV, 90-95), just as they are prodigal of all life; and in the symbolic world of the *Odyssey*, it is not very far from their excessive eating to their threats on the lives of Telemachus and Odysseus. In both areas the Suitors are rebellious against order, contemptuous of man and nature (and of the gods, too: they do not pray or sacrifice before they eat). Their presence in Odysseus' palace, with their games, their dances, and their incessant banqueting, gives Ithaca its Saturnalia; Odysseus will rudely interrupt their Carnival, rout these Lords of Misrule, and restore the authority and sanctity of royal power.

Here in Book I Homer first shows us the Suitors at play and at table. Although he picks up this note of feasting in the later books of the poem, notably XVII-XX, the banqueting is gradually contaminated and undermined by the doom awaiting the Suitors. Homer neatly preserves the image of the meal in foreshadowing the the sudden, bloody end of their carousals on Apollo's feast day at the end of Book XX. "It was certainly a rich and savoury dinner that they had managed for all their merriment to prepare, since they had slaughtered freely. But as for their supper, nothing less palatable could be imagined than the fare which a goddess and a strong man were soon to spread before them" (391-93). This note is picked up again at the very end of Book XXI when Odysseus has shot the arrow through the axes. As he is about to reveal himself to the dismayed Suitors, he tells Telemachus, "The time has come now to get their supper ready, while it is light, and after that to pass on to the further pleasures of music and dancing, without which no banquet is complete" (428-30). Next, the slaughter of two of the Suitors is set against the appropriate backdrop of banqueting, which recalls Agamemnon's banquet-death. Antinous drops his cup as he is hit and "his foot lashed out and kicked the table from him; the food was scattered on the ground, and his bread and meat were smeared with gore" (XXII, 17-20). As Eurymachus falls, he knocks over the table and "lurching across the table, he crumpled up and tumbled with it, hurling the food and wine-cup to the floor" (XXII, 83-86).

So in death the Suitors spill and befoul the very food they stole in life, their ill-gotten feasts cut short by the unexpected arrival of the host.

Just before this terrible denouement the emphasis had been on drinking, for when it became clear that the Suitors could not at once string the bow, Antinous interrupted the contest to have drinks poured out by the stewards. Then, when Odysseus suggested that he be given a try at the bow, Antinous instantly accused him of being drunk and cited for him the riotous wedding feast of the Centaurs and the Lapiths, where Eurytion the Centaur got drunk and tried to kidnap Peirithous' bride. The initial irony here—the wedding feast that turns into a brawl is about to take place in Odysseus' palace—is compounded by the fact that the action of the *Odyssey* does climax with a wedding feast of sorts, the mock wedding staged to conceal the news of the Suitors' deaths (XXIII, 133-35) just before Odysseus reveals himself to Penelope.

So much, then, for Homer's emphasis on food. The *Odyssey* is, as Fielding observes in *Tom Jones* (IX, 5), "that eating poem," but it is Homer's genius to make so mundane an activity as eating and so familiar a scene as the dinner table reinforce the theme and structure of his poem. Food is the stuff of life, a necessity for survival and continued life, and it is the fact that Odysseus accepts life's deprivations without despairing of survival or slackening his effort which is his distinguishing virtue, his *areté*. Furthermore, one of the poem's central themes is that the place of eating, the banquet, the scene of peace and the bond of fellowship, is menaced by the intemperance of the Suitors and restored by the hero Odysseus.

VII

Telemachus caught sight of Athene and set off at once for the porch, thinking it a shame that a stranger should be kept standing at the gates. He went straight up to his visitor, shook hands, relieved him of his large spear and gave him cordial greetings. (I, 118-122)

When Athena arrives in Ithaca she is greeted by Telemachus and offered hospitality with all the grace and generosity that the young prince can muster. At once we note here and will see repeated throughout the poem a concern for the forms of polite life. The observance of elaborate formalities is one of the rituals of heroic, or feudal, life, and the *Odyssey* is, for all its bloodshed, a very courteous poem (and a very clean one, too, if one considers the frequent bathing).[6] Attention to the niceties and ceremonies of manners is important in the society of the *Odyssey*, and Menelaus is justifiably enraged at the beginning of Book IV (30-36) when a servant asks if he should perhaps send on Telemachus and Peisistratus for someone else to entertain. Odysseus' famous speech to Nausicaa in Book VI (149 ff.) is almost incredibly mannered; and before Alcinous accepts the suppliant Odysseus in Book VII, Homer has Echeneus, a Phaeacian elder, remind him of the obligations of hospitality (159-66).

The *Odyssey*'s interest in the proprieties relates mostly to hospitality, of which an important element is the giving and receiving of presents. The giving of gifts seems so much a part of the rituals of hospitality that it is a distinct jolt in Book XIII (14-15) to hear Alcinous say that the Phaeacian leaders will get back through a special tax the worth of the gifts they have given to Odysseus. One does not expect this kind of rude directness in a poem so civilized that even a monster like the Cyclops can be generous: "I will eat Nobody last, and the rest before him. That shall be your gift" (IX, 369-70). When even the savage Polyphemus can claim to be kindly, the boorishness of the Suitors throughout the poem, but especially in Books XVII and XVIII, deserves special note; and it is appropriate that a question of manners should seal their fate. The question, in Book XXI, is whether Odysseus, still disguised as a beggar, should be allowed to try to string the bow. Penelope says, "Antinous, it is neither good manners nor common decency to show such meanness to people who come to this house as Telemachus' guests" (XXI, 312-14). But the Suitors never get the opportunity to show even this much common decency, for Eumaeus hands the bow to Odysseus over their noisy protests. Here we see an extra dimension to the threat the Suitors have embodied throughout the *Odyssey*. Not only do they want to marry Penelope and slay Odysseus and Telemachus, but they also want to undermine the whole façade of heroic manners. Because they are without courtesy, regard, tact, or restraint, they would utterly de-civilize Ithaca. This is a society (and a poem) in which manners are important because they buttress conduct and give life style, grace, and ease; in a formalized society they can heavily influence men's lives by providing them with traditional and approved patterns of action. All of this the barbarism of the Suitors would despoil. Indeed, their threat to Odysseus—father, husband, and rightful king—is much like that of Odysseus' other great opponent, Poseidon. Like the Suitors, Poseidon can discomfit and disconcert Odysseus through his wrath and unruliness, because like them and like his native element, his power is violence, an assault more on the order and conduct of life than on life itself (for he cannot kill Odysseus). Hence the bad manners of the Suitors are more than a source of irritation to Odysseus and they deserve more than disapproval from the reader of the *Odyssey;* in their total impoliteness the Suitors truly represent the forces of death, since by their loutishness and their squandering they would destroy the kind of civilized life that the *Odyssey* celebrates.

VIII

Yes, if only Odysseus, as he then was, could get among these Suitors, there'd be a quick death and a sorry wedding for them all. (I, 265-266)

The reader of the *Odyssey* is quickly impressed by the various ways in which the Suitors are bad. Still the question lingers: are they—all of them—bad enough to be so summarily executed? A difficult question, for in dealing with the Suitors Homer had to make them meaningful characters both individually and collectively—they are, after all, princes of Ithaca and thereabouts and privileged to court Penelope—and yet justify their wholesale slaughter in Book XXII. The Suitors must have presented Homer with almost as serious a problem as they offered Odysseus, and it was very likely a problem not of Homer's making. The Suitors were probably a fixture of the *Odyssey* story, inherited by Homer from some primitive version of the myth in which the returning hero found them courting his wife and promptly massacred them with the simple unconcern of a mighty warrior;[7] or they might be relics of a folk tale of the fortunate "suitor" (in this case Odysseus) who wins the hand of the "princess" (Penelope) by defeating his rivals, perhaps with the help of his magic bow. But the innocent mayhem of saga or folk tale cannot subsist in the humane and sophisticated world of Homeric epic, particularly in the *Odyssey* with its emphasis on the ideal of justice. To make the deaths of the Suitors expected by us and deserved by them is both aesthetically and morally necessary; and Homer takes pains, early and late in the poem, to do just this. He begins, first of all, by establishing that the Suitors represent no real threat to Odysseus.

The listener has been led to infer from the very beginning of the poem that Odysseus will prevail. Mentor-Athena says that if Odysseus should appear at the door armed with helmet, shield, and two spears—as he does at the beginning of the spear-combat—the fate of the Suitors would be swift and their wedding bitter (I, 255 ff.). When Odysseus returns they will pray for fleetness of foot (I, 164); they actually flee like frightened cows, or a flock of birds before vultures (XXII, 299-

307). Heaven has promised success to Odysseus, both by omens (XX, 102-21) and by the mouth of a seer (XX, 351 ff.), and Athena has pledged him her support; but no divinity at any time favors the Suitors. Their leaders are slain at the beginning of the slaughter; the others have only their daggers, weapons for close combat, which their fear of the mighty bow makes them avoid. In the spear-combat the number of spears in the hands of the Suitors is so small that the odds are fairly even—twelve spears to eight—and Athena makes ineffective those which are cast by the Suitors.[8]

In this way Homer can dispose of the physical menace of the Suitors, even without the intervention of Athena, whose part in the battle is wisely limited; furthermore, by having the Suitors lose their leaders in the first round of the battle, he makes understandable the desperation that leads to the final bloodbath. Still, it is difficult to prevent some sympathy from going to the Suitors. The simile Homer uses to describe their panic—"They scattered through the hall like a herd of cattle" (XXII, 299)—may hint at the animality of their lives, but it is more suggestive of the helplessness of their plight and the piteousness of their death. It is well, therefore, to review the role of the Suitors from the beginning of the poem and see how Homer builds his case against these one hundred and eight young men.

In Book I, even before the Suitors appear, we hear of Aegisthus, who committed the same crime the Suitors will attempt and was killed in retaliation by Orestes. That it is Zeus who cites Aegisthus disapprovingly in his short disquisition on crime and punishment strengthens our expectation that the Suitors can expect little better from the hands of Odysseus. For the rest of Book I the Suitors perform but briefly—"Each man voiced the hope that he might share her bed" (366)—in their nominal role as wooers of Penelope. Instead of expanding on this aspect of their function in the poem, Homer presents them both directly in their speeches and indirectly in Telemachus' complaint to Athena as interested less in Penelope than in enjoying the wealth of Odysseus and anticipating their prospects for kingship. Their great number (recorded as 108 in Book XVI, 247-53) and the viciousness of the few who are individualized (Antinous is cruel, Eurymachus deceitful; only Amphinomus shows some moderation)[9] also suggests that they have more in common with each other than with Odysseus or Penelope, thereby lending substance to the impression many critics have that the Suitors would replace the heroic kingship by an oligarchy, a political development that did, in fact, occur in Greece after the Bronze Age.

In the debate of Book II the issues are made clear. Telemachus makes a formal appeal, "in the name of Olympian Zeus, in the name of Themis, who summons and dissolves the parliaments of men" (68-69), first to his fellow Ithacans for relief from the Suitors (with little success; mythology has few examples of popular indignation, and the citizens of Ithaca seem little involved in what is happening in their king's palace), and then to the Suitors themselves "to quit my palace and feast yourselves elsewhere" (139). Telemachus' second speech is followed by an omen interpreted to forebode "a bloody doom for the Suitors one and all" (165-66) and by statements from Eurymachus and Leiocritus that are remarkable for their rashness and violence. Eurymachus, in abusing the seer Halitherses, is sure that Odysseus has died already and Leiocritus, in attacking Odysseus' old friend Mentor, is sure that he will die once he gets home. These overt threats to Odysseus' life have followed the Suitors' depradations of his property and culminate at the end of Book IV where Antinous organizes a party to ambush and assassinate Telemachus as he returns from Sparta. Although this attempt is unsuccessful, in Book XVI Antinous, the worst of the Suitors (and, appropriately, one of their leaders), again urges that Telemachus be put to death. In Book XIV Odysseus learns from Eumaeus of the Suitors' plan to assassinate Telemachus, and he can reflect on this knowledge during the long scenes of his abuse by the Suitors in Books XVII to XXI. So, however gory may be the Suitors' death, Odysseus need show no mercy to men who have tried to kill his son, the heir presumptive to the throne of Ithaca, and who would try to kill him too if they were given the opportunity. Indeed, without detracting from Penelope's attractiveness, it is a misnomer to call them Suitors; they should rather be called Usurpers, since it is their main design to weaken Odysseus' household, break or destroy his family, and thereby win supreme power in Ithaca for one or more of their number.[10] There is no custom that requires the presence of the Suitors in Odysseus' palace, for as Antinous admits in Book XVI (390-93), each of them could court Penelope from his own house. But by feasting in Odysseus' house they can not only enjoy themselves at another's expense but they can also diminish Odysseus' resources and, by extension, weaken his position as king. Nor will they give up their presumptuous claims even if Odysseus were to return, for by Leiocritus' threat in Book II they make it clear that if Penelope will not acknowledge herself a widow they will make her one. So when Odysseus faces the Suitors, all one hundred and eight, in Book XXII, he is only incidentally a husband rescuing his wife; he is much more a king fighting to preserve his throne from illegal and unworthy successors, and he is above all a man fighting to save his life.

IX

> The goddess spoke and the next moment she was gone, vanishing like a bird through a hole in the roof. (I, 319-320)

When Athena first appears to Telemachus in Book I she is disguised as a Taphian chieftain named Mentes, and when she leaves him toward the end of the book she "vanishes like a bird through a hole in the roof." This unexpected metamorphosis of a character already disguised points to another quality of the *Odyssey* that is as characteristic of its hero as it is of the gods—sudden change. The varieties of changes in the *Odyssey*, whether by divine transformations or by simple disguises, constitute what might be called the metaphysic of the poem: change and permanence. In part this is inevitable in a poem laced with the tall tales of folklore which traditionally feature magical changes and uncanny disguises. But Homer does not limit himself to the use of change as a complicating factor of the plot. Change itself becomes one of the perils confronting Odysseus, and if he will triumph it is because he can weather change as he weathers the relentless sea, because he can reach the relative stability of Ithaca while keeping his identity intact in the process.[11] Amidst the shifting shapes of the wondrous world he traverses, Odysseus himself has an irreducible reality and a fast grip on the permanence of experience. He is tempted to linger, and he does; he is tempted to forget, but he does not, for he always remembers who he is—a man and not a god, and a man who has a wife, a son, and a home. Like Auden's traveler, he sees the strangeness:

> Of lands where he will not be asked to stay;
> And fights with all his powers to be the same
> The One who loves Another far away
> And has a home and wears his father's name.[12]

In these terms of change and permanence the central image of the poem is the myth of Proteus, for from him one can learn the truth only by holding fast through all his changes and by persisting until he returns to his original shape. In the same way the stubbornness of Odysseus' resolve to return home will preserve him from despair in the face of repeated frustrations and will eventually reward him with the vision of his reunited family. In the process of this return, however, Odysseus himself is subject to change. There are two great scenes of change, described in identical lines, one before Nausicaa in Book VI and the other before Penelope in Book XXIII. Both are performed by Athena upon Odysseus as he emerges from a bath, epiphanies of a wholly regenerate hero after the batterings of the sea and the Suitors, respectively. These are less scenes of transformation than of restoration, their subject less a new Odysseus than the old Odysseus, the true Odysseus, handsome and godlike, as he must have looked before getting involved in the long unpleasantness at Troy. As his reward for endurance and self-preservation, Athena recreates him. Less flattering, but far more functional, is the change in Book XIII (429-38), where Athena withers and ages Odysseus and disguises him in the rags of an aged beggar so that he can make his way unobserved in Ithaca. This disguise is not consistently maintained throughout the second half of the poem, being discarded in the Irus incident, for example, in Book XVIII. It is finally shed (the rags, at least) at the beginning of Book XXII when Odysseus strings his bow and squares off against the Suitors.

The reader should be aware that disguise is itself a species of change, and disguises are resorted to often in the second half of the poem. Odysseus masks his identity behind lies—not simple evasions of the truth but elaborate and tedious stories in which he usually passes himself off as a Cretan. To Athena in Book XIII he represents himself as the murderer of Idomeneus' son; to Eumaeus in the next book he is the son of a wealthy Cretan named Castor; to the Suitors in Book XVII he describes himself as a once wealthy man maltreated by Zeus; to Penelope in Book XIX he turns out to be Idomeneus' brother; and finally his father Laertes hears that he is a native of the mysterious "Alybas." For good measure Eumaeus is told in Book XIV of a fictitious attack on Troy in which Odysseus participated as third in command to "Odysseus" and Menelaus. Add to this the famous "Nobody" incident, and we have a poem in which the hero parades under false pretenses through most of the action.

The combination of lies, disguises, and sudden metamorphoses is most important for the special effect of the *Odyssey*. The changes they entail illuminate the quality of action in the poem, the shifting, perilous world with its multiple distractions and its fateful discrepancies between reality and illusion—a world where beggars are kings and wooers are killers. To cope with this world, to exploit its resources, to bend its vagaries to the heroic will requires more than good intentions. It requires the practical wisdom of an Odysseus, his wit and his cunning and his doggedness. Likewise, the lies and disguises that Odysseus resorts to define his character (can one imagine Achilles, in the *Iliad*, disguising himself—or Ajax lying?) and reinforce the impact of his personality. Odysseus is defined by negatives; he assures us so often of what he is not that his eventual unmasking has the impact of a divine revelation. Because the problem of identity is climactically important in the final books, Odysseus takes great pains to impress on Ithaca the power of his personality, to distinguish himself from others, to assert his uniqueness and superiority. This is one explanation of the tests and trials in the *Odyssey*. Odysseus' feats at the Phaeacian games, Odysseus doing in Irus, Odysseus stringing his bow in competition with the Suitors, Odysseus slaying the Suitors while Athena rations her assistance "to put the strength and courage of both Odysseus and his noble son on trial" (XXII, 237-38), Odysseus' suicidal word play with Polyphemus—all revelations of the special strength and individuality of Odysseus. His appearance to Telemachus in Book XVI (179-85) is so blinding that Telemachus turns away in fear that this is a god before him. His final revelation to Penelope is no less characteristic of the poem, being precipitated by her testing him. There seems almost a touch of sadism in the scene with Laertes in Book XXIV where Odysseus tells the last of the poem's lies to his poor father, but once again Odysseus cannot afford to make Laertes' recognition easy. The truth must be learned by suffering if it is to be appreciated, just as the return to Ithaca cost Odysseus many a heartache. (Identity is typically associated with suffering even in the first half of the poem: Telemachus' tears in Book IV [114] interrupt Menelaus' reminiscences and reveal his identity; Odysseus' tears at VIII, 550, prompt Alcinous to ask him his name.) For Odysseus to have merely returned after twenty years would be a relief and a joy to his family, but a twenty-year absence tends to dull the edge of loss. Odysseus is out to sharpen this edge, to intensify the shock of his return by heightening, but only temporarily, his family's agony of privation.

These mythical metamorphoses and the problem of identity that they pose also assist the poet when his material seems to be failing him. After the great interest of Odysseus' wanderings in Books V to XII, there is a distinct slackening of dramatic tension in the last dozen books. This abatement of interest is at least partially redeemed by the suspense of Odysseus' gradual unmaskings—for one of the truest techniques of storytelling is to ask who is the mysterious stranger. There is a technical problem here too. Odysseus must be alone in the center of the stage if his presence is to have the startling effect appropriate for the return of the hero. But no sooner is

Odysseus back in Ithaca, arrayed as a beggar, than he finds himself implicated in an intrigue to disarm the Suitors and slay them. This involvement, with its petty details and squalid characters like Irus and Melantheus, could detract from the reader's interest in Odysseus, were it not that Homer had manipulated his main characters in such a way as to enhance the personality of Odysseus. *Odysseus' family becomes Odyssean.* Telemachus is now matured and "heroized"; he has become a replica of his famous father. Penelope, too, restrains herself from rushing into the arms of her husband. Instead, she tests him in proper Odyssean fashion, with a self-control and cunning that must have warmed Odysseus' wary old heart. Always a "wise" woman, as her characteristic epithet shows, she has here acquired the wry skepticism of her husband. Philoetius and Eumaeus are also involved with Odysseus, but they are convenient blanks. So, despite the crowded scene in the final books, Homer has succeeded in conveying the absolute dominance of Odysseus, his saturation of character and action. That the importance of his person is not accidental is proved by no less a personage than Athena herself, who at the very end of the poem calls Odysseus by his royal titles.[13] Odysseus has preserved his identity, first as a man against the witches and monsters of the adventures and then as a husband against the Suitors, and now his identity is confirmed by the full acceptance of his status in Ithaca. The returned hero has become the great king.

X

It is too sad: it never fails to wring my heart. For in that catastrophe no one was dealt a heavier blow than I, who pass my days in mourning for the best of husbands. (I, 341-44)

Here Penelope has heard the bard Phemius sing of the *Nostoi*, the "Returns" of the heroes from the Trojan War, and in tears she asks him to choose another theme for his song. Many who went to the Trojan War did not return; and the most poignant lines in the *Iliad* are reserved for the deaths of those young men who left families behind them and for the family of Hector, Andromache, and Astyanax that was destroyed in the course of the Trojan defeat. Again in the *Odyssey* Homer takes a family for his subject, and he reminds us over and over again that the primary relationship of his poem is that of a broken family: Odysseus separated twenty years from his wife, a stranger to his son, the cause of his father's abdication. The main action of the poem's first four books is a son's search for news of his father, as that of most of the subsequent books is a father's return to his family. But Odysseus' is not the only family in the poem. The whole Heroic Age is seen in its family setting; whereas the *Iliad*, as Nilsson points out,[14] showed us the family life of the gods, the *Odyssey* shows us the family life of the heroes. First Telemachus comes upon Nestor with his sons, and later Nestor's own Peisistratus is sent as his companion to Sparta. There they find Menelaus celebrating the weddings of his son and daughter and they later meet Helen herself. The tragic lady of the *Iliad* is a striking index of the shift in emphasis in the *Odyssey*. The glory and the dream have fled, and what is left is the slightly bourgeois scene of Colonel and Mrs. Menelaus at home in the manor house. Further on, Nausicaa has her mother and father and five brothers, whose clothing she washes. Aeolus keeps his family intact by marrying his children to one another and then throwing continual banquets to celebrate this tidy arrangement. In the Underworld of Book XI Odysseus meets his mother and learns of his family. The heroines who approach him are introduced by Homer as "all the women who had been the wives or the daughters of princes" (XI, 227). Agamemnon tells Odysseus of the hard luck he had with his wife Clytemnestra and then inquires about his son. Achilles asks for information about his son and father. Then, throughout the second half of the poem, Odysseus gradually reunites his family by appearing successively to Telemachus, Penelope, and Laertes.

This concern with families, with the ties that bind them and the forces that disrupt them, extends in the *Odyssey* to Homer's most characteristic literary device, the simile. Critics have often remarked how few overt similes there are in the *Odyssey* as compared with the *Iliad*. (One reason for this is obvious: the similes in the *Iliad*, with their vignettes of animals, farm, and nature, vary the monotony of the battle scenes, whereas the scenes of the *Odyssey* are already picturesque and diverse.) Two of the *Odyssey*'s similes, or, rather, one twice told, deal with home and family. Menelaus uses it in a speech to Telemachus in Book IV, and it is repeated by Telemachus to his mother in Book XVII. "It is just as if a deer had put her little unweaned fawns to sleep in a mighty lion's den and gone to range the high ridges and the grassy dales for pasture. Back comes the lion to his lair, and hideous carnage falls upon them all. But no worse than Odysseus will deal out to that gang" (IV, 335-40, and XVII, 126-31). The oddness of comparing the bloodthirsty Suitors to unweaned fawns makes this simile all the more striking. This family simile prepares for many others of the same order. In Book V, 394-99, Odysseus' seeing land is compared to children's seeing their father recovering from illness. In Book VIII, 523-30, Odysseus hears Demodocus' songs of Troy and weeps as a wife weeps for her husband fallen in battle. When Odysseus returns from Circe to his men in Book X, 410-17, he is reminded of cows welcomed from pasture by their happy, frisking calves. Odysseus longing for home in Book XIII, 31-35, is compared to the ploughman eager in the evening to drag his tired legs home. Eumaeus greets the returning Telemachus in Book XVI, 17-21, like a father welcoming back an only son after a nine-year absence. The tearful reunion of Odysseus and Telemachus in XVI, 216-18, is compared to birds whose nests have been robbed of their young. In XIX, 518-23, Penelope compares her own decision to the turns of song of Aedon, who killed her own son Itylus. In XX, 14-16, Odysseus' rage at the behavior of the Suitors' mistresses makes him snarl like a bitch protecting her puppies from a passing stranger. In XX, 61-78, Penelope prays to Artemis that she may be snatched away by the storm winds just as were the daughters of Pandareus, who had been robbed of their parents by the gods and left as orphans. These examples make us aware of a radical change from the *Iliad* to the *Odyssey*. No longer needing similes for change of pace and mood, Homer now uses them thematically to remind us at random points in the story that this is a poem about a family. Similes like these conspire to give the action of the *Odyssey* an intimacy and immediacy that balance the more exotic folklore materials and stress in familiar terms the importance of Odysseus' return, the wholeness and stability he achieves by reestablishing his family, and the prosperity his reunited family assures his land.

By the end of Book I we have seen the gods in council and Odysseus' family in Ithaca. We have met Athena, Telemachus, Penelope, and two of the chief Suitors, Antinous and Eurymachus. We have yet to meet Odysseus, who will not appear until Book V, but we know what and whom he is returning to. It is important that we know this early, and by beginning the poem in Ithaca, in Odysseus' home, and not, say, on Calypso's island, Homer establishes at once that Odysseus is a returner and not a wanderer.[15] The gods may neglect Odysseus occasionally in his adventures, but here in Book I Zeus and Athena are united in wanting to bring him home, just as Penelope and Telemachus are united in needing him at home. Book I also begins to tell us what kind of poem Homer is composing. The *Odyssey* is a civilized poem, and its themes are the themes of all great literature—love and justice. Odysseus is the loving father and husband and also the just king. The values he embodies are the values that keep all men humane—hospitality, good manners, loyalty, intelligence, patience. Odysseus' name may have become synonymous with curiosity and enterprise, but everything that is good in the world of the *Odyssey* takes place within families; the villains of the poem are the loners, like Polyphemus, or the mobs, like the Suitors, and were Nausicaa without a family on Phaeacia she would only be a paler version of Calypso. Furthermore, the *Odyssey* is an optimistic poem—perhaps too easily optimistic in its vision of a world where the good and the bad get their due. But Homer does not minimize the world's hazards or the perverseness of man or god; even Zeus, the god of hospitality, can encourage Poseidon in his petty retaliation against the kindly Phaeacians in Book XIII. Finally, the *Odyssey* is broad and inclusive; it is an *epic* poem, not in the *Iliad's* way, with men and nations massed in the first conflict of East and West, but epic in its comprehension of all conditions of men—good and bad, young and old, dead and alive —and all qualities of life—subhuman, human, and superhuman, perilous and prosperous, familiar and fabulous. The Greek critic Longinus described it as an "ethical" poem, a word that Cicero later explained (*Orator* 37, 128) by a definition that could well be applied to the *Odyssey*—"adapted to men's natures, their habits and every fashion of their life."

⋖ II ⋗

TELEMACHUS AND
THE *TELEMACHEIA*

The criticism of Homeric epic has become so formalized over the centuries that it has developed denominations to accommodate scholars of various persuasions. There are, first, the "Separatists," who believe that the *Iliad* and the *Odyssey* are by two different poets, who may not have even known of each other's work. Then there are the "Analysts," who believe that different poets worked on different parts of the two poems at different stages in their evolution, with "Homer" being credited with whatever was most meritorious in this process. Opposed to the analytical critics are the "Unitarians," who maintain, with varying degrees of persistence, that one poet—whom they agree on calling Homer—composed both poems. Complicating this division is the fact that few of the adherents to any of these sects have ever held the faith pure, and the quarrels within and between them have long provided the scholarly world with controversies that were sometimes diverting but more often dispiriting. Recent research into the ways of composing oral poetry has weakened the meaningfulness of these labels,[1] and the angry and abusive essays once written in defense of one or another of these views have now acquired a quaintness never intended by their authors.

When the Analysts dealt with the *Odyssey* (and they always dealt very harshly with the *Odyssey*), it was one of their standard truths that if Books I-IV of the poem were not by another hand, then they were certainly distinct enough in treatment and integration to deserve a special name—the *Telemacheia*. The books of the *Telemacheia*—along with Book XV, which tells of Telemachus' return—are separate from the poem in that they are generally concerned with Telemachus, Odysseus' son. Telemachus is an important character in the *Odyssey*.

Telemachus appears in sixteen books of the *Odyssey*, in all except V-XIII . . . and he speaks more often than any other of the characters in either poem, except their respective heroes . . . Telemachus also furnishes the incentive for the plot of the Suitors, which both emphasizes their *hybris* and increases the interest as we approach the climax of the story. In fact, the Suitors, without Telemachus, lose half of their importance, just as there would be no tragic outcome of the Wrath if there were no Hector. And, finally, a lonely, tearful, vacillating, and altogether human Penelope would be impossible if there were no Telemachus or his equivalent; she would have to be more decisive and energetic—more the queen, and less the woman.[2]

Certainly the Telemachus we meet in Book I has his problems in Ithaca, but his position in the *Odyssey* raises problems for the poem too. Either the political structure of Ithaca is highly irregular or else Homer has left much unsaid about the conditions of kingship there. First of all, why is not Odysseus' father Laertes king of Ithaca? He is still alive, and we meet him in the last books of the poem out in the country where he has withdrawn in sorrow over the loss of his son, but even before his retirement he does not seem to have ruled as king.[3]

The dilemma in which this situation involves the Ithacans is obvious. On the one hand, old Laertes has been made unfit for kingship, presumably through infirmity; on the other hand, Telemachus is unqualified because of youth and inexperience. Since strength and vigor seem the qualifications for rule in Ithaca, the people are victimized by the weakness of their leaders—the weakness of old age and of youth, the senility of Laertes and the adolescence of Telemachus. Odysseus alone combines exuberance and experience, and he is desperately needed. It is noteworthy, too, that when he returns not only does he save his family and his land, but the vitality of his presence extends to his father and his son. For Laertes there is a sudden and miraculous transformation. "Athena herself intervened to increase his royal stature. As he stepped out of the bath she made him seem taller and sturdier than before, so that his own son was amazed when he saw him looking like an immortal god" (XXIV, 368-71). Athena's powers here show symbolically how the presence of his beloved son has revitalized the aged Laertes. In the same way, the Telemachus whom Odysseus meets in Book XVI and fights beside in XXII is not the young man whom Athena found in Book I; but if his transformation is gradual, it is because not even a goddess can immediately infuse into a young man the wisdom accumulated in a lifetime's experience as hero and king. Where Laertes had, like Odysseus, already known the meaning of the heroic life and needed only to be rejuvenated, Telemachus must be introduced, or initiated, into it. The process of this introduction, this initiation, is one of the purposes of the four books (and part of

Book XV) commonly referred to as the *Telemacheia*. In a society, like Ithaca, where kingship depends not so much on inheritance as on merit, it is not enough for Telemachus to have the title of prince; he must be prepared to prove his worth, as he will in Book XXII, but before the crucial test comes he must know what it is he is fighting for. Pylos and Sparta, the two cities he visits in Books III and IV, can offer him the examples he will need of heroic civilization. Hence we should understand these opening four books of the poem as educative—as Telemachus' preparation for heroism.

The *Telemacheia* properly begins after the Council of the Gods when Athena visits Ithaca to hearten Odysseus' son and urge him to call an assembly of Ithacans and then set off to Sparta and Pylos in search of news about his father. Here she finds a despairing Telemachus lost in the dreamworld that has become his since the Suitors made the real world intolerable. He is hoping that somehow Odysseus will appear "from somewhere" (115). It will be Athena's purpose in the next few books to rid Telemachus of his melancholy, to show him how in the heroic world dreams can be translated into realities. Although the goddess is at once impressed by Telemachus' physical resemblance to his famous father, his insecurity is such that he is even unsure of his own identity and never refers to his father by name.[4] "My mother certainly says I am his son; but for myself I cannot tell" (I, 215-16). It will be the burden of the next few books to harmonize Telemachus' inner and outer selves, to make him be his father's son not merely in name but in deed. The example Athena offers him is of another famous son, from the Agamemnon myth. "You are no longer a child: you must put childish thoughts away. Have you not heard what a name Prince Orestes made for himself in the world when he killed the traitor Aegisthus for murdering his noble father? You, my friend—and what a tall and splendid fellow you have grown!—must be as brave as Orestes. Then future generations will sing your praises" (I, 297-302). This encouragement by Athena—to be repeated by Nestor in Book III—is not without its effect, but Telemachus' adolescent attempts to take charge are a fiasco. He shocks Penelope quite unnecessarily, even cruelly, and then turns on the Suitors in a tone of voice that must have been totally unexpected by them, for at first they are taken aback. "This is sheer insolence" (368), he says, using the Greek word *hybris*, and they bite their lips in astonishment at his boldness. But the new Telemachus lapses back into the old Telemachus as soon as Antinous, one of the Suitors' ringleaders, has a chance to distract him. Poor Telemachus discourses vaguely on the nature of kingship, then is so uncertain of his own position (if, indeed, he is to succeed

Odysseus) that he concedes the claims of the other princes. He then concludes lamely that he intends at least to control his own house. This has not been a very convincing display of newly found authority or spirit, but in his confusion Telemachus has at least raised the great question which Odysseus will answer: Who is to be king of Ithaca? He has also asked what kingship means; and his tentative answer—an enrichment of one's house and an increase of honor (392-93)—will soon be confirmed in the glory and wealth of the courts of Nestor and Menelaus. Thus, in this book, Telemachus has been awakened by Athena to an awareness of royalty and its prerogatives. This is important, for it is his initial preparation for the coming struggle to preserve the same prerogatives of rightful kingship in Ithaca. When the first book ends with the quiet and touching scene of Eurycleia tending Telemachus as he prepares for bed, Homer has completed the picture of Telemachus' surroundings. He is in some way subject to Penelope, although he has now dared to bridle at her authority; he is attended by an aged nursemaid; and he is bedeviled and oppressed by insolent Suitors. Father Odysseus is away, grandfather Laertes is off on his farm, and Telemachus has only two women to support him against the menace of a hundred and eight young men determined to marry his mother and take over his father's throne.

In Book II we read little that particularly convinces us that Telemachus has profited by Athena's encouragement. He denounces the Suitors at a public assembly and appeals, without much hope, to their nonexistent sense of justice. When he then goes on to invoke Zeus and Themis, we feel that this is clearly not the kind of speech his father would deliver, and whatever faint effect it might have had on the hard hearts of the Suitors is dissipated when he concludes his words with a sudden burst of tears. The crowd pities Telemachus, but the Suitors do not, particularly the cynical Antinous, who goes on to shift the blame to Penelope for her funeral-shroud ruse. Once again Telemachus' attempt at oratory has been abortive and ineffective, but once again he has raised a central theme of the *Odyssey:* the justice of Odysseus, the injustice of the Suitors. As spokesman for his family, and speaking in an assembly of the citizens of Ithaca, Telemachus has publicly arraigned the Suitors for their crimes against his father's household, an indictment that will still obtain when Odysseus seeks a terrible swift vengeance in Book XXII.[5] Furthermore, the terms of his speech, just as in Book I, foreshadow elements of experience in Books III and IV. He describes Odysseus' kingship as fatherly in its gentleness (47), and he will see gentle and exemplary fathers in Nestor and Menelaus; the food squandered by the Suitors in their incessant parties in Ithaca (55-56) will be consumed in order and harmony at the feasts in Pylos and Sparta; the wine that intoxicates the Suitors in Ithaca (57) will become a tranquilizer in Sparta; and the weakness Telemachus protests here (60-61) will be overcome by confidence and resolve before he sees Ithaca again.

After his speech Telemachus commences his preparations for his journey, but runs into the astonished protests of his nurse Eurycleia: "But there's no need at all for you to endure the hardships of wandering over the barren sea" (369-70). This feminine attraction to place is partly what Telemachus must overcome by becoming acquainted with the ways of the heroes who did suffer hardships at Troy and then had to return over the seas to the great centers of the Mycenaean Age. But for all Telemachus' determination, Eurycleia's objection still stands, and to assert that Telemachus must rid himself of inhibitions induced by the women who have brought him up is not a very convincing justification for his trip. Indeed, the fact that Telemachus intends to go off on a junket at this crucial time, with the Suitors growing impatient and poor Penelope at her wit's end, was duly noted by Analyst critics and made one of their reasons for believing in the original separateness of the *Telemacheia*.[6] In this objection they were anticipated here by Homer himself,[7] by Odysseus at XIII, 417 ("Do you want him too to scour the barren seas in misery while strangers eat him out of house and home?"), and by Eumaeus in XIV, 178 ("Suddenly some god deprived him of his wits—or perhaps it was a man who fooled him—and off he went to holy Pylos on his father's trail").

They are right—this does seem like the worst conceivable time to leave Ithaca. To them the answer is provided by Athena in XIII, 422. Yes, she could have told Telemachus the truth about his father, but she sent him off to win what the Greeks called *kleos,* reputation, a hero's highest reward: "I myself arranged the journey for him, in order that he might win a noble *kleos.*" The fact is that nothing Athena *told* Telemachus would have had any lasting effect; what he needed before meeting his father was experience in heroic society, the kind of experience he had never known in Ithaca, and this journey to two of the great centers of heroic civilization, Pylos and Sparta, was the only way he could gain it. To put it in religious terms, Telemachus had to be baptized into the heroic life, to commune with its leaders, and to be confirmed in its values, or he would never be a trusted ally to his father or a fit successor to the kingship. *Kleos* ranks with *aretê,* excellence, as an honorific word in the heroic vocabulary, and it is only in places like Pylos and

Sparta that Telemachus can absorb their meanings and prepare himself to merit them. It is true that this is a critical juncture in the affairs of Ithaca, but far from impeding Telemachus, it makes his journey all the more necessary. For it is at the truly critical periods of man's life—when he is most exposed—that he must appeal to an extra source of strength, an access of grace. Hence Telemachus' journey is neither unnecessary nor unmotivated, for the necessity is Telemachus himself—his youthfulness, his inexperience —and the motive transcends the averred search for information.

The beginning of Telemachus' journey is particularly significant. It is traditional in primitive societies for the young candidate to be taken at night from the care of the women, either forcibly or without their knowledge, and given over to the elders of the tribe who will conduct the tests and trials by which the novice must prove his worth and fitness as a member of his tribe. In the same way, Telemachus leaves in the dark of night, his mother Penelope unaware of his departure and his nurse Eurycleia bound by an oath not to reveal the reason for his absence.[8] He is accompanied by Athena who is disguised as Mentor—a name that has come into English as the word for teacher or coach. The first stage of their journey is Nestor's citadel at Pylos. Here we are in the heroic world and we notice that Telemachus does not know how to act, what to do, how to approach the great man. "Remember that I have had no practice in making speeches; and a young man may well hesitate to cross-examine one so much his senior" (III, 23-24). Athena encourages him, tells him not to be so shy, to rely on his native wit, and to have faith in the assistance of the gods. It is she who passes the cup to Telemachus as the libation is being offered and it is she who offers a prayer that Telemachus can repeat after her. Telemachus manages nicely in his first bout with the social forms of a kingly court, though not as deftly as Nestor's son Peisistratus, who had, after all, the benefit of growing up within this mannered society. (And how polite they are, as Homer here as elsewhere emphasizes manners and ceremony.) Nestor then delivers a long speech— he rarely delivered a short one—luxuriating in the recollected sorrows of the Trojan War and remarking Telemachus' resemblance to his famous father. (We notice here the continuing reference to faithful sons—Antilochus, Peisistratus, Orestes.) In reminiscing about Troy, Nestor passes from Achilles to Ajax to Patroclus and finally to his own son Antilochus. He praises Odysseus for his good sense, tells how, out of allegiance and piety, Odysseus stayed behind at Troy with Agamemnon, and does not forget to remind Telemachus approvingly of the sterling example of Agamemnon's son

Orestes. Telemachus picks up the hint, but then awkwardly blurts out his despair of ever seeing his father again "even if it proves to be god's will" (228), for which he is promptly chided by Athena, who gives him a one-sentence lesson in the power of the gods. In the fully integrated society piety and manners are identical and Telemachus must learn to trim his private doubts accordingly. That evening Athena leaves and Telemachus is received into Nestor's palace where he sleeps beside Nestor's son Peisistratus. The next day Nestor arranges an elaborate banquet for Telemachus' crew and even has his youngest daughter, Polycaste, give Telemachus a bath. This might seem an odd way to honor a guest, but in the intimate and domestic setting of this book it is both appropriate and charming. At any rate, to continue with religious terminology, it acts almost as a kind of baptism, for out of it Telemachus emerges, "looking like a god" (468). Nestor then gives him horses and a chariot and sends Peisistratus to accompany him on his way to Sparta. Athena is no longer with Telemachus, but he has been accepted into Nestor's household, bathed by his daughter, and is now being escorted by his son. For Telemachus this brief visit to Pylos has been a tonic experience after the noisy desperation of his life at Ithaca, and at last he is ready to break out of the shell of his depression and uncertainty and to make his way in broad heroic society.

Book IV opens with a scene of feasting and family cheer in the splendid palace of Menelaus, where King Menelaus is celebrating the marriages of his son and daughter. Here in Sparta there is a prosperity, a security, and a family intimacy that Telemachus had never known in Ithaca and had only lately met in Pylos. Again we are aware how subtly and exactly Homer chooses details to contrast Menelaus and Sparta with Odysseus and Ithaca. The primary complication of the *Odyssey* is the disunion of a family, whereas here we have an immediate awareness of union (the double marriage) and reunion (Helen). And compare the joy and harmony of Menelaus' banquet with the pointless carousing of the Suitors. Nor has anything in Telemachus' limited experience prepared him for the magnificence of Menelaus' palace, before which even Peisistratus is impressed. Nevertheless, Telemachus is making progress; at the beginning of Book III the mere sight of a hero panicked him; here he seems quite sure of himself before Menelaus, and he can be forgiven his awe before the royal palace—after all his father, who has seen everything, is no less impressed by Alcinous' palace in Book VII. Manners are once again stressed: Menelaus' anger when a servant suggests the possibility of sending Telemachus and Peisistratus "on for someone else to entertain" (29), and his embarrassment when Telemachus weeps as he reminisces of Odysseus. And in the stories Menelaus tells there are little morals which can also be of use to Telemachus. Proteus, for example, tells Menelaus that he should have sacrificed to Zeus before embarking; Ajax's fate is an example to those who would blaspheme; and when Proteus tells Menelaus of what happened to Agamemnon and then urges him to hurry back to his land as quickly as he can, Homer shows us that the point is not lost on Telemachus. He refuses to protract his stay in Sparta, and when Menelaus offers him three horses he has the wit and the temerity to ask for a gift he can carry, not horses which are so impractical on Ithaca. Menelaus is impressed.

Book IV (along with Book XIV) has generally found little favor with critics of the *Odyssey.* Admittedly, Menelaus, the cuckolded warrior of the *Iliad,* is not much more interesting in the *Odyssey* as a slightly blowsy rich man, and some of Helen's radiance has diminished in her translation from the walls of Troy. But the Homer of the *Odyssey* rarely likes to compete with the Homer of the *Iliad,* a fact which has led some Separatist critics to posit two Homers. The Nestor of Book III does not quite sound like the Nestor of the *Iliad,* who so often compared the debased present with the glorious past of his own young manhood, and the domestic calm of Menelaus' menage in Book IV should not be troubled by memories of old loves and old hates. Only Helen still feels the rankling memory of that old infatuation, "shameless creature that I was" (145), but she shows a proper remorse and has equipped herself with a drug that has "the power of robbing grief and anger of their sting and banishing all painful memories" (220). But it is all to Homer's purpose to deflect the attention from these commanding figures of the *Iliad,* because the center of these books is Telemachus. For him and for the whole poem Book IV is effective and meaningful; it not only extends the *Telemacheia,* but it also prepares the reader for Book V, easing him, as it were, into the *Odyssey* proper.[9] For Menelaus' fate closely approaches Odysseus', since his return was recently as uncertain as is Odysseus' now. Menelaus is also proof to Telemachus and to us that even after the weariest of journeys one can return home safely and enjoy a happy and prosperous future. Further, Menelaus' range of experience is considerably broader than Nestor's, extending beyond the known Greek sea routes into the areas of the fabulous where creatures like Proteus live. It is only from this strange Old Man of the Sea that fairly specific information about Odysseus is available, and this information is, after all, the purpose of Telemachus' trip. Also, the Proteus episode is just the sort of adventure Odysseus might have had, and thus the Nestor-Menelaus-Proteus progression prepares us for the fantastic adventures of Books V to XII and gives us a richer view of Odysseus than if we had first seen him when Hermes was sent to Calypso. Proteus' advice to Menelaus to return home as quickly as possible is also a warning that Odysseus and Telemachus have no time to lose either. The accounts given in Books III and IV of the returns of the various heroes are also deftly arranged by Homer to isolate Odysseus' situation. Nestor was one of the first to return, Menelaus one of the last; Ajax, son of Oileus, was killed off the coast of Asia Minor, Agamemnon after his return home. In this milieu of rescue and death, all possibilities are exhausted except one, which transcends them all—Odysseus' fate—of travels compared with which Menelaus' were child's play, of the multiple threats of death in the distance still to be covered, of a home and family near ruin, as was Agamemnon's, and of the loss of ship and company. Odysseus still belongs neither to the saved nor to the lost, and he can perish like Agamemnon or he can come safely home to peace and quiet like Menelaus and Nestor. With the latter he is connected by his wisdom, with the former by his wanderings, with both by the divine favor he enjoys. But yet Odysseus surpasses them all in ways that the *Odyssey* will describe and for which the *Telemacheia,* and particularly Book IV, has prepared us.

Before the *Odyssey* proper begins with Odysseus on Calypso's island in Book V, the scene changes to Ithaca where the Suitors hatch their plot to ambush and slay Telemachus and where Penelope hears from the herald Medon about Telemachus' trip and also about the Suitors' designs on her son. The transition from Sparta is abrupt, but again we notice how everything in the poem returns to Ithaca—Odysseus from his wanderings, Telemachus from his trip; and now, just before Odysseus appears, Homer returns us to Ithaca for a final glimpse of what Odysseus is returning to—homicidal Suitors and a suffering Penelope. It is this impression of home and wife—and not of Helen and Menelaus—that we have when we first see Odysseus in the next book.

The last scene of what we can still call the *Telemacheia*—that is, before Telemachus meets his father and they both challenge the Suitors—takes place in Book XV, when Athena again visits Telemachus, this time in Sparta, and urges him to hasten back to Ithaca. His reaction is almost as precipitate as it was in Book I, but Peisistratus checks him; after all, there are proper ways to do these things, and "a guest never forgets a host who has shown him kindness" (54-55). Telemachus is impatient, and he frets through Menelaus' moralizing and the rituals of gift-giving, but by now he is aware of his responsibilities and feels himself a man of action; now it is more than he can stand to have to return to Pylos to brave Nestor's oppressive hospitality. Telemachus has been schooled in the forms of the heroic life in Books III and IV; in XV he has earned the right to transcend them. He can now dispense with social obligations, for his own obligations are infinitely more demanding. He must be about his father's business.

The last scene of the *Telemacheia*, the Theoclymenus episode, is puzzling. Why is Theoclymenus brought in? Perhaps to palliate murder in the face of Odysseus' subsequent treatment of the Suitors? Certainly Theoclymenus, like Odysseus, can say, "It is my fate to wander about the world" (XV, 276), for he is being pursued by the kinsmen of the man he has slain. And for the rest of the poem this relic of the feuds of the heroic world will hover uneasily in the background like Conrad's Leggat, the secret sharer in Odysseus' revenge and a disturbing reminder of the random violence and blood guilt of the heroic age. But for Telemachus the decision to accept Theoclymenus demonstrates his newly won authority: he has the right to give asylum, even hospitality, if he wants, to a murderer. Through Theoclymenus Homer can underscore the identity of Telemachus, show that he is now coming into his own and can afford his father the assistance Odysseus might have received from another Achaean hero on the fields before Troy. In this sense it is appropriate that the *Telemacheia* end with Theoclymenus interpreting an omen, a hawk appearing on the right with a dove in its talons, which he sees as signifying that, "No family in Ithaca is kinglier than yours; you will have power forever" (533-34). As a professional performance this is indeed shabby, and as a prophecy it is so vague as to be meaningless. But it is not a prophecy; it is an accolade, a ceremony to complete the *Telemacheia* by marking Telemachus' attainment to true manhood. His doubts about his right to his royal patrimony are allayed, and he is rewarded with an assurance of future success. Theoclymenus' words signal an access of power that Telemachus will need in the days ahead.

Telemachus now returns to Ithaca.

> On the voyage from Ithaca to Pylos, Telemachus was as he himself said only a passenger. . . . He had little to do either with the preparation of the cargo or the sailing of the ship; everything was under the immediate control of Athena; but on the return trip he was the sole commander and cared for all matters which concerned both ship and crew with the assurance of a veteran seaman.[10]

After Telemachus is back in Ithaca his fortunes merge with those of his father and his role is clearly subordinated to Odysseus'. This somewhat diminishes the impact of Telemachus' personality, and Homer is not always successful in giving him something to do. Although he is potentially his father's most powerful ally against the Suitors, even Odysseus seems to ignore him when he tells Athena, "I am alone" (XX, 40). Of course, Telemachus shows his mettle: only a nod from Odysseus in Book XXI keeps him from stringing the bow, and he seems to do his share in the fight with the Suitors. He is exceptional in his mercy, checking Odysseus from slaying Phemius the minstrel and Medon the herald, and relentless in his revenge, personally stringing up the unfaithful serving women. (Perhaps his savagery toward the servant girls, like his occasional harshness with his mother, is part of a deep-seated reaction against an adolescence spent among women.) But if Telemachus does acquire some of his father's heroism, it is at the price of his own individuality. Homer seems conscious of this and goes to great lengths to let us know that Telemachus is still around. But the glimpses he gives us are often of the "old" Telemachus, laughing (XXI, 105), sneezing (XVII, 541), and absentmindedly botching his father's plans (XXII, 154); Telemachus speaks out of turn (XXIII, 97-103), parades in borrowed feathers.

One answer to the problem presented by Telemachus' role seems to be that the second half of the *Odyssey* belongs to its hero alone. As we saw in Chapter I, Odysseus, so long absent and so often disguised, must dominate the action of the final books, both by the vitality of his own presence and by the revivifying effect he has on his family. Penelope subjects Odysseus to one more trial, devising a test—the bedpost ploy—her husband could be proud of. Later on, this transformation also affects Laertes, who, as we have noted, is rejuvenated by Athena. Telemachus, for his part, becomes so like Odysseus that he is indistinguishable from him, being so much a replica of his father as his own name (Far-fighter?) is—or sounds like—a title for Odysseus.[11] The problem Homer faced was technical: how to show the maturity, individuality, and heroism of Telemachus without detracting from the dominance of Odysseus. If his compromises were not always successful, it is largely because the pre-logical situations of myth will not readily conform to the logic of literature.

Yet even though Telemachus yields place to Odysseus in the final books of the poem, in his own "epic" he can stand a thorough comparison with his more famous father; and at the same time we can see how skillfully Homer uses the *Telemacheia* as a kind of "little epic" to balance and contrast with the rest of the *Odyssey*. First, both Telemachus and his father make journeys, from which both must return home indirectly and in constant danger. Odysseus has to survive the world's perils and disorders while preserving his identity and his purpose. For Telemachus the world is precisely the opposite, centering in the well-ordered kingdoms of Nestor and Menelaus. Telemachus' progress is from the chaos of Ithaca to the cosmos of Pylos and Sparta; Odysseus seeks the stability of his home across the ragged edges of the world—he must go, literally, through hell and back. Furthermore, in their separate worlds there is an important difference between the two: Odysseus acts, Telemachus reacts. Although Odysseus, in his struggles with giants and monsters and witches, more than once comes within an inch of his life, Telemachus' experiences, apart from the social, are vicarious—he listens, observes, absorbs. He learns about his father—not his whereabouts, but rather the full story of the Odyssean exploits at Troy. He can now better appreciate his father (particularly when it comes to infiltrating a hostile city), because he has learned of his derring-do from the greatest living authorities on heroic *aretê*.

It is important, therefore, that in this atmosphere of wartime heroism recollected in the tranquility of peace Telemachus do nothing, just as it is for Odysseus in the Underworld of Book XI. And yet, through his own faltering efforts to make this trip and share the memories of Nestor and Menelaus, Telemachus is able to rehearse privately many of the great crises of the *Odyssey*. The stories of the heroes fighting at Troy and returning to Greece prepare him for the coming struggle by expanding his knowledge, if not his experience, of the world. He sees two families, those of Nestor and Menelaus, that are as happy as his own is unhappy; and when he visits with Helen he sees a woman who suffered for love as bitterly as his own mother Penelope is suffering. He hears of a prophet Proteus who is much like the prophet Tiresias whom Odysseus meets in the Underworld (Book XI), and yet this Proteus is at the same time a sea monster like those who threaten his father; and, finally, he too must hurry home at the warning of Athena to save Penelope from the Suitors. Homer has succeeded in packing a version of the *Odyssey* into a little more than two books, all in the passive voice.

In the *Telemacheia* Telemachus frees himself from the women who have reared him, the Suitors who harass him, and the island that inhibits him, and visits a world that is rich and new. Within the scope of the whole poem the adventure of Odysseus that most nearly corresponds to his son's journey is in Book XI, where Odysseus visits the Underworld. This adventure, called the *Nekyia* in Greek, may not be one of Homer's best efforts, but it does define the special quality of the *Telemacheia* and it is interesting to compare them. Both of these episodes, for example, presume to show us the hero learning something vital to his future welfare, yet in each the information is either not forthcoming as supposed or else could have been acquired elsewhere. Further, it is only in the *Nekyia* that Odysseus assumes the stance of Telemachus in Books III and IV— that of the passive observer of an unfamiliar ceremony. However, there are significant differences. Whereas Telemachus is introduced to the heroic tradition in the front parlors of the returned chieftains where manners saturate conduct, where worldly prudence and social maturity have a climactic importance, and where the storms and struggles of life seem comfortably remote, Odysseus on the other hand has to break through the world's surfaces, has to pass, indeed, from life to death. Telemachus hears about Agamemnon and Achilles; Odysseus goes to see them. Odysseus' fate is cosmic; hence he must penetrate to the mist-bound areas beyond this life. His living presence in Hades prefigures the life that he will restore to the stricken land of Ithaca. Odysseus must go beneath the levels of the world, the very levels which Telemachus must come to know with tact and nicety. Ordinarily Odysseus is satisfied with his knack for survival in a hostile and perplexing world, but in the *Nekyia* he is in touch with powers beyond his techniques and he is immobilized by them. He comes for specific information from Tiresias, but he stays to meet the ghostly representatives of the heroic Establishment. Odysseus needs no education in the ways of this world; now his experience has been deepened by exposure to the ways of the next world. But if the *Odyssey* in Book XI breaks through the forms of life, the *Telemacheia* is content to slide along their surface, initiating its young hero into the rites of a faith in which he was born but never reared. Its high priest is Nestor, its catechism the legends of Troy.

The escorts of the two heroes are another point of contrast. For much of his return Odysseus is saddled with the burden of his company, the responsibility for their safety and the accountability for their lesser talents. Within his larger fate are subsumed the fates of his companions. With Telemachus, however, the situation is reversed—Odysseus has men under him; Telemachus has men over him, for he is under the divine protection of Athena and the fraternal guidance of Peisistratus. Since Odysseus either overshadows the men who accompany him or else travels alone, his personality everywhere dominates the action even when the forces opposing him are most critical or catastrophic. Telemachus does not dominate the action; instead he is usually at its mercy. He finds himself in social impasses, situations where he fears that his training and experience are not adequate. He is never alone; Athena and Peisistratus are ever with him, and his final character is shaped by their initial tutoring and example. Their salutary presence, their promptings, assurances, and commendations are the background of his development.

From the time of Porphyry, who called it a *paideusis*, or "education," the *Telemacheia* has sometimes been taken as a kind of *Bildungsroman*, or "novel of education"; and it is true that all the elements are there. Telemachus at the beginning is the callow youth; Pylos and Sparta are the open world; Athena is the guide, the mentor. And the result is Telemachus beside his father fighting with skill and courage against the Suitors. It is not simply an education, though. What Telemachus experiences is not something taught, but something imparted—one young man's initiation into a world he has inherited and whose values he will soon have to defend by force. (One notices that what one would most expect to happen fails to materialize—namely, that either Nestor or Menelaus would volunteer to send off a detachment of their palace guard to Ithaca to restrain the Suitors, protect Penelope, and confirm Telemachus in his patrimony. Instead they seem to assume that this is exclusively the problem of Telemachus and Odysseus.) And yet it is not a rite of initiation in the anthropological sense of a set of artificial dangers contrived to test a candidate's reactions. Growing up fatherless in a house recently occupied by scheming Suitors has given Telemachus a taste of danger; now, in the *Telemacheia*, Pylos and Sparta demonstrate to him the possibilities of peace, and the examples of Nestor and Menelaus expose him to the precedents of heroism. In a sense, then, the *Telemacheia* is a kind of reverse *Bildungsroman*, because it exposes the young hero not so much to danger as to safety. Telemachus' life was already perilous enough back in Ithaca; now in Pylos and Sparta he has a vision of peace, security, happiness, and family reunion, all the values he has never known but will soon have to win back in a bloody and desperate battle. Goethe named the hero of his *Bildungsroman* Wilhelm Meister to foreshadow the master he would become; likewise there is something appropriate in the sound of Telemachus' name, "Farfighter," so apt for this young Ithacan who in the not so far future will be the kind of fighter his father can trust and admire. For in the final books of the *Odyssey* Telemachus will meet his greatest trial, the challenge to prove his worth by successful deeds, to demonstrate before his elders and his peers that he is truly the son of his father. For Telemachus the meetings with Nestor and Menelaus are sacraments, the visible means to the graces of heroism. Hence the search he makes is for more than news of his father: he seeks the social and family assurance of the heroic age, where sons are like their fathers because they have grown up in their shadows, as Antilochus was like Nestor, or where sons inherit their father's bravery and defend their memories, as Orestes avenged the death of Agamemnon. Telemachus has never had a father to provide the scenes and cues for his glory, and so this journey is not only for information but, as Athena admits (XIII, 422), to win him his first *kleos*. Since Homer's time the fatherless child has been a major figure in Western literature—Oedipus, Hamlet, Stephen Dedalus, Dickens' waifs—because the quest for the father reflects the profounder theme of the spiritual condition of children deprived of faith and security. Telemachus leaves the menace of the Suitors behind in Ithaca, experiences the harmony and stability of Pylos and Sparta, and then returns to help his father purge the contaminated land and restore justice and the social conventions. The heroic society Telemachus traverses is an enclosed world with its own laws and conventions and ceremonies, its own mystique of wisdom and virtue, its own concept of honor. Out of it emerges a new Telemachus. For the meaning of these five books, the final purpose of the *Telemacheia* is to delineate the birth of a hero. As such it parallels in its way the *Odyssey* proper—which presents the return of the hero and, with Laertes, the rebirth of a hero—and thereby completes the picture of heroic life which the *Odyssey* celebrates.

⋅⋅§ III §⋅⋅

ODYSSEUS IN WONDERLAND

In the first section of his poem, the *Telemacheia,* Homer introduced
to us the figures whose lives will be most deeply affected by Odys-
seus' return, and he gave Odysseus' son a series of adventures, if one
wishes to call them that, which prepare us by contrast for the sub-
ject of Books V to XIV, Odysseus' own adventures. These are the
stories of Odysseus that everyone seems to know—the Cyclopes,
Calypso, the Lotus Eaters, and so on. Whenever the *Odyssey* is
abridged, these are the stories usually left intact, and whenever
selections are made from the *Odyssey* these are the stories usually
excerpted. This gives the reader of excerpts or abridgements a lop-
sided version of the *Odyssey* and leaves him with the impression
that this great epic poem is an absorbing adventure story, fascinating
in the way fairy tales are fascinating, but hardly worth the at-
tention of serious readers who, if they are that interested, can turn
back to the *Iliad* or forward to Greek tragedy for the terror, the
beauty, and the drama of Greek literature. This inordinate interest
in the adventures is a great injustice to Homer and the whole
Odyssey, because it is likely that in this section of the poem he was
least original. Of course, in the absence of Homer's sources, it is
unwise to speculate about originality, but the recurrence of adven-
tures much like Odysseus' in the mythologies of other lands suggests
that in Books V through XII Homer is taking common folk tales,
well known stories of witches and demons and monsters, and using
them to put Odysseus through his paces, to give him an array of
adventures in the wide, wild world of the folk tale. After Odysseus
gets home, in the final books of the poem that are the subject of
the next chapter, much of the action is taken up with the nasty
carryings-on of the Suitors and the elaborate preparations by Te-
lemachus and Odysseus for the massacre. Likewise, in the first four
books of the poem Homer was confined to the heroic world as it
opened up before the eyes of a young man of limited background
and awareness. Now, between those two sections in which the ac-

45

tion is limited and the poet has local and specific concerns come the eight books of the adventures; and here Homer can indulge himself in actions and characters that are unusual and unpredictable and in descriptions of a world that is far and fantastic, unreal and unknown. It is a world of colors, smells, and shapes that one never finds in the *Iliad,* for instance, or in the other books of the *Odyssey.* Sometimes Homer's descriptions are of a landscape that is lush and abundant, like the black poplars and the violets and the bubbling springs of Calypso's isle at the beginning of Book V, or the eternal fruits and heavy dark olives that never fail to grow in Alcinous' orchard in Book VII; sometimes Nature is violent, like the storm of Book V that tears Odysseus' skin as it batters him onto the rock ledges of Phaeacia; sometimes the descriptions are surrealistic, like the meat of the Cattle of the Sun in Book XII which suddenly comes alive and crawls and groans on the spits as Odysseus' men are about to eat it; sometimes detailed and realistic, like the boat-building of Book V; or sometimes just fantastic, straight out of never-never land, like the gold and silver watchdogs that guard Alcinous' palace in Book VII, or the floating island of the Winds in Book X, or Scylla in Book XII, with her twelve feet and her six long necks.

This is not strictly the world of epic or saga in which heroes lead great armies or fight one another in personal combat or found cities. This is the world of the folk tale, not too far removed from Jack and the Beanstalk or Sleeping Beauty or Rumpelstiltskin—a world out of time and place in which the hero pits himself and his all-too-human resources, his wit, his courage, his skill and cunning, against the monster and the dragon and their weapons of power and magic. It is noteworthy that although Odysseus has his problems in these books as he does in other parts of the poem, here—at least in the wanderings of Books IX to XII—he does not have Athena to help him. She shows up now and again among the Phaeacians, but one feels that Homer is bringing her in to remind us that she is still around, and, in general, she is not of much help to Odysseus. There are a number of reasons for this. It was part of the heroic tradition that the Achaeans returning from Troy were punished by Athena for having failed to discipline Locrian Ajax after he had invaded her temple and assaulted her priestess Cassandra during the sack of the city. According to the tradition Odysseus shares in this punishment, but according to the *Odyssey* myth he must be assisted by Athena. Homer tries to circumvent this difficulty by minimizing the extent to which Odysseus is implicated in Athena's retaliation. Four times the poet adverts to Athena's wrath, but at I, 327, the reference is generalized; at III, 135, it is directed against Agamemnon and Menelaus, and Athena is not even mentioned by name; at IV, 502, it is directed at Ajax alone; and at V, 108, in the closest reference to Odysseus' involvement, Hermes avoids naming him and says that his companions were lost but Odysseus himself was saved.

By Book V we have already been supplied with a different reason for Odysseus' plight—the wrath of Poseidon, mentioned specifically by Zeus at the beginning of the poem and to be recounted in detail by Odysseus in Book IX. Poseidon's wrath may not be as convincing as Athena's (for one thing, it does not explain Odysseus' troubles before he left the island of the Cyclopes, and for another, Polyphemus, who sinned so grievously against the *Odyssey*'s prime virtue of hospitality, deserved the punishment he got from Odysseus[1]), but at least it helps Homer establish Athena as Odysseus' champion, even though he did not choose to go against the tradition by having her actively assist him in his difficulties in Books IX to XII. Another reason for keeping Athena out of these books is that they tell, by flashback, of adventures that predate the Council of the Gods in Book I where Athena officially announces that her concern for Odysseus is so pressing that she now demands divine acquiescence and cooperation in bringing him home.

> If we knew that Athena assisted Odysseus during his wanderings, we should wonder why she had taken no interest in the affairs of Ithaca during the ten years which precede the action. We gain the impression that she has neither watched over Telemachus, nor comforted Laertes, nor kept Anticleia from grieving to death because of the absence of her son. She suggested to Penelope the contest of the bow; yet, although she is the goddess of spinning and weaving, she did not, as far as the poet lets us know, inspire the stratagem of the web: the Suitors give Penelope the credit for the trick, and the queen herself says it was "heaven" that put it into her breast. The truth is that the poet's manner requires him to keep Athena out of the story until the opening of the poem, and to be consistent he must not permit her to help Odysseus on his wanderings. The gain from this is considerable. The adventures are more thrilling than if Odysseus were under the constant protection of Athena, as Telemachus is on his journey.[2]

A final reason for Athena's absence may lie in the kind of stories told in these books. This world of the folk tale is older than the world of the gods and heroes, and Homer may here be drawing on an independent tradition that predates the stories of Troy and the myths of the Heroic Age. It would be inconvenient, then, to insert Athena into situations where she did not belong and where she could only deflect interest from Odysseus, who, we must remember, is telling the story in the first person.

The fact that Odysseus himself relates most of these folk-tale adventures makes them different from much of the rest of the *Odyssey* in tone and point of view, but they are by no means haphazardly designed. Quite the opposite; Homer seems to have absorbed himself in their composition, for the adventures have a scheme and a shape in Books IX through XII that are not always evident in other sections of the poem. Structurally, two short sections, two short adventures, are followed by one long. Cicones—short; Lotus Eaters—short; Cyclopes—long. Cattle of the Sun—short; Sirens—short; Scylla and Charybdis—long. Again, relatively mild adventures are spaced between the darker, more violent adventures: Cicones, harsh; Lotus Eaters, mild; Cyclopes, harsh; Aeolus, mild; Laestrygonians, harsh; Circe, mild; Scylla and Charybdis, harsh; Sirens, mild; and Cattle of the Sun, harsh.[3]

The adventures also tend to fall into three general categories of peril. First, irresponsibility (Lotus Eaters, Sirens, and Phaeacians), those who try to make Odysseus forget Ithaca and Penelope, try to tempt him to stay with them and give up his ties to home and family and country. Second, sex (Circe and Calypso), women who boast their superiority to Penelope, who even offer Odysseus immortality if he will stay with them as a kind of captive lover. The third category is violence (Cicones, Laestrygonians, Cyclopes), subhuman creatures whose interest in Odysseus does not go beyond destroying him and his men. Irresponsibility, sex, violence—typical dangers confronting man in the world.

One may wonder here if all this is perhaps meant allegorically. Can the *Odyssey*, or at least this part of it, be a kind of Greek *Pilgrim's Progress?* Certainly the adventures can be made to yield one or more allegories. "The Lotus Eaters represent the temptation of exotic food, the Cyclops the menace of savage anger, Circe the allurement of strange vices." [4] Just as Christian in Bunyan's *Pilgrim's Progress* is the pilgrim who must make his way from the City of Destruction to the Celestial City and who must avoid all the pitfalls along the way—places like Vanity Fair and Doubting Castle, and people like Mr. Worldly Wiseman and the Giant Despair—so one can perhaps imagine Odysseus as a kind of pre-Christian hero who must make his way from Terrible Troy to Happy Ithaca by way of Calypso, Circe, the Cyclopes, and the Land of the Dead. Odysseus can be made a prototype of the human soul in its journey through this world of darkness and danger, and the early Christian Fathers went so far as to compare Odysseus with Christ.

The difficulty in allegorizing the adventures is that the allegory does not work. There are little problems like the Circe episode, where we may be tempted to allegorize Circe as passion and then explain her turning men into swine by the animalizing effects of unbridled passion. All well and good, except for one pesky detail: Homer tells us explicitly that when the men who had been turned into swine were turned back into men again, they "looked younger and much handsomer and taller than before" (X, 395-96). This would seem to suggest that this change was not all bad, that to go through this transformation and emerge from it can be a salutary experience. A second objection to Homeric allegory is more fundamental. The allegorist usually begins with a thesis or moral and then invents characters and situations to fit the various qualities he wants to demonstrate. This is not the way of Homer, who avoids conceptions and abstractions, and celebrates the specific, the concrete. Homer cannot deal in abstractions because he does not have the words to express them—it took the Greeks centuries of thinking and talking to make their rudimentary terms for goodness and justice and honor supple and abstract enough to serve the uses of philosophy. The Homeric style, rich in its concrete nouns and verbs and poor in abstractions, can dispense with general terms because it describes these terms in action. Homer need not theorize about honor when he has written an entire poem, the *Iliad,* about one man's defense of his honor. In the *Odyssey* he does not talk about fidelity, but instead portrays Penelope, a faithful wife; he has no word for justice, but the whole poem is about the injustice of the Suitors and the just punishment they receive at the hands of Odysseus; he never knew the word "responsibility," but one portion of his poem is devoted to the gradual awakening to and acceptance of responsibility by the young Telemachus. The simplicities of Homer are in his style, the profundities in the acts and issues his style renders, and in neither style nor substance can his poems be segmented into the crude equivalents required by allegory.

The Adventures, or Wanderings, of Odysseus open in Book V with a speech by Athena to Zeus and the other gods repeating word for word what Mentor said to the Suitors in Book II—namely, that Odysseus was a just king and loving father. There are other repetitions in her speech. When she speaks of Odysseus' being stranded on Calypso's island, she is repeating Proteus' words to Menelaus in Book IV (557-60), and when she announces that Telemachus has gone to Pylos and Sparta for news of Odysseus, she is repeating Medon's words to Penelope near the end of Book IV (701-2). Now it is the way of oral poets to repeat themselves. They work, charac-

teristically, not with words but with formulas, parts of lines, lines
or groups of lines, that they can vary to describe the typical scenes
that recur in their poems. Once a formula has been developed it can
(though it need not) be repeated as long as it applies, just as the
thoughts Athena expressed here had been formulated earlier in the
poem. This kind of repetition is a primary convention of oral poetry,
and the reader of Homeric epic must be aware of its existence and
quality if he is to free himself from certain expectations developed
from modern novels and be able to read a poem like the *Odyssey*
with an informed understanding. Moreover, these repetitions (when
they are not effaced by translators who surrender to the modern
impulse to variety) have a subtle effectiveness, in that they provide
a stable background, a kind of security. In the *Odyssey*, for example,
the preparation, serving, and consumption of food, so often expressed
in formulas, reminds us of the permanence of simple human ac-
tivities in a world of wonder and peril. In the present instance, the
repetitions in Athena's speech, which deal with obvious and intro-
ductory matters (and would be of good use to a rhapsode beginning
his recitation with this part of the poem), hardly disturb the ordi-
nary reader, and he would probably be surprised to learn of the
controversy they have provoked or the unkind words ("so great an
abuse of the poet's license, so insensitive a treatment of his materials
. . . an abnormally artificial patchwork" [5]) uttered against them.
This speech may not be Homer's finest, but it has its uses. First, a
subsidiary section of the poem has ended, or, rather, has been sus-
pended, and the main business of the *Odyssey*, its hero's return, is
about to begin. Since Athena will not be directly involved in
Odysseus' account of his adventures, it is well that we are reminded
of her concern for Odysseus, which she here expresses before all the
gods. It is well, too, that Homer has her quote Mentor's words on
the love and justice of Odysseus. Love and justice are the themes of
the poem, they are embodied in Odysseus as father and king, and
from this time forth Odysseus' fortunes will be the central subject
of the poem.

Zeus decides in Athena's favor and sends Hermes off to tell Ca-
lypso (whose name means "Concealer" in Greek) to let Odysseus go.
Calypso tries to be hospitable to Hermes when he arrives, but this
self-important divinity sniffs at his country cousin and treats her
like a poor little nymph from the woods. Zeus' command is relayed
to Odysseus, whom we first see "sitting disconsolate on the shore in
his accustomed place, tormenting himself with tears and sighs and
heartache, and looking across the barren sea with streaming eyes"
(82-84). When Calypso assures Odysseus that she will let him go,

she renews her offer to make him immortal if he will relent and promise to stay with her for all time. Odysseus' answer is significant for the poem. He acknowledges that Penelope, as a woman, is inferior to Calypso. But Penelope is his wife, she keeps his home, and Odysseus insists on returning home—though without ever expressing any love for Penelope. Homer tries here, and elsewhere, to minimize any romantic interest, because he is in touch with the love of husband and wife that is profounder than sex or romance. It is what the Greeks called *philia*, a word best translated as "attachment." Odysseus' return to Penelope is a quest for wholeness, a need for union, and the word Homer uses most often, as he does here, to describe Penelope, "wise" or "prudent" Penelope, explains her attraction for Odysseus. Odysseus' travels are cyclical, away from Ithaca to Troy and now back to Ithaca, but the spiritual direction of the poem is centripetal, "inwards, homewards, toward normality." [6]

Of course, this does not mean that Odysseus cannot take his time; in fact, he spent seven years with Calypso, and the irreverent have often asked why, if he was in such a hurry to get home, did he not pack up and leave after a month or so. But the great tension of this section of the poem is between Odysseus' fixed purpose to return home and his unflagging curiosity, impulsiveness, and receptivity. It is true that he is going home, but he does not want to miss a thing—or a gift—on the way, and he wants to make very sure that the people he meets remember that he is none other than Odysseus, son of Laertes, king of Ithaca, hero of the battle of Troy, and the cleverest man in all Greece. This desire for public recognition, standard for men of the Heroic Age, was considerably inhibited by the seven lonely years of concealment with Calypso. This is Odysseus' longest disappearance in the course of his journey home; it is his most protracted inactivity; and it is paradoxical that he is kept from leaving Ogygia by a love that is both more and less than Penelope's. Scholars have speculated on what, if any, occult significance the Calypso incident may have. In the chronological order of Odysseus' adventures, which differs from the order in the poem, the sojourn with Calypso occurs directly after the sin against the sun god and in the days when all myths were interpreted as solar myths this was taken as the period in the progress of the year-spirit when he is hidden, his powers enfeebled, waiting only for his time of return. Whatever the exotic source of the Calypso tale, it is hard to see it bearing this much significance in the poem that we read, and it is much less important for Odysseus than his next adventure, with the Phaeacians.

Odysseus leaves Ogygia by building a boat with tools that Calypso somehow makes available to him, though one likes to think that Calypso otherwise never laid hand to axe, drill, or adze. But once on the sea the king of Ithaca is exposed to the wrath of Poseidon, who returns from his visit to the Ethiopians to discover the mischief that has been created in his absence. He blasts Odysseus' little boat and Odysseus has to crawl ashore, naked and battered, onto the island of Scherie, the land of the Phaeacians. Phaeacia is the last of Odysseus' adventures and the only one to be described directly by Homer. Athena also appears in this episode—awakening Nausicaa at the beginning of Book VI and persuading her to go and wash her clothes at the beach where Odysseus is sleeping; taking the form of a young girl at the beginning of Book VII to guide Odysseus to Alcinous' palace; next disguising herself as a herald at the beginning of Book VIII to assemble the Phaeacian leaders for the entertainment arranged for Odysseus the next day; and, finally, marking the length of Odysseus' discus throw at the Phaeacian games. The triviality of Athena's activities here (apart from her appearance to Nausicaa) suggests that Homer is making work for her and that Phaeacia, in its outward customs so much like a recognizable Greek community, is still half in a fairyland that does not admit of gods and heroes—just as Odysseus here will be physically close to the reality of Ithaca, but still, in the stories he tells in Books IX to XII, imaginatively immersed in the unreal world he has just left. For Odysseus, his "return to the Phaeacians is thus a major step in the return to humanity. For different as their way of life is from Ithaca, it is still recognizably human. Scherie thus forms an essential steppingstone from the complete suspension of Ogygia to the complete involvement of Ithaca." [7]

The relative normalcy of the Phaeacians is best represented by the first of them Odysseus meets, the very young and very charming princess Nausicaa. One of the most unforgettable scenes of the poem occurs now, at the beginning of Book VI, when the girls are playing ball and their shouts awaken the shipwrecked Odysseus. Rising unsteadily to his feet and all swollen with bruises and streaked with brine, he staggers out from the bushes, naked as the day he was born and very likely the last thing these girls expected to see on wash day. All but Nausicaa run away terrified, and Homer gives us this very dramatic confrontation between a fragile young girl and a battered old hero. In a poem that celebrates the civilized life and turns on matters of form, there is no more delicate and sensitive social situation than this. Odysseus responds magnificently with perhaps the most mannered speech (especially 149-69) in all Greek literature. It is contrived, ingratiating, sincere, totally appropriate, supremely effective. He asks, "Are you some goddess or a mortal woman?" The two possibilities: "If," on the one hand, "you are one of the gods who live in the sky, it is of Artemis, the Daughter of Almighty Zeus, that your beauty, grace and stature most remind me." The specific example, with the implication that her beauty is "slender, virginal, athletic, in contrast . . . with the more voluptuous charms of Aphrodite." [8] "But if," on the other hand, "you are one of us mortals who live on earth, then lucky indeed are your father and gentle mother; lucky, your brothers too." The deftly sentimental appeal to Mom and Dad, the cautious assurance that he knows she has brothers to protect her from strangers. "How their hearts must glow with pleasure every time they see their darling join the dance!" Again Nausicaa is associated with her family. "But he is happiest of them all," we note the logical progression, "who with his wedding gifts can win you for his home." A bold stroke, this, to allude so directly to Nausicaa's being unmarried, but Odysseus protects himself by taking a new tack. "For never have I set eyes on such perfection in man or woman. I worship as I look." The next general statement, redeemed by the mention of worship (sebas), and followed by the specific example: "Only in Delos have I seen the like, a fresh young palm-tree shooting up by the altar of Apollo, when my travels took me there." Odysseus compliments himself and reassures Nausicaa. Odysseus is not only well traveled but pious, and he then goes on to cap this with nostalgia, "with a fine army at my back that time," and finally fish for sympathy, "though the expedition was doomed to end so fatally for me." Nausicaa is now to understand that this savage apparition before her was once a great general, but is also a sensitive man, who can remember, "How long I stood spellbound at the sight, for no lovelier sapling ever sprang from the ground." A general who can keep the troops waiting near a shrine while he admires a sapling is truly a soldier with a soul. If any speech at all is possible for a naked hero in front of a young girl, then Odysseus has made it, and when he goes on to tell her his troubles and beg her assistance, we know that Nausicaa knows that this is the kind of man she can bring home to mother. Which is precisely what she does, introducing Odysseus, and us, to the wonderful world of the Phaeacians.

A reader of the *Odyssey* can easily be of two minds about the Phaeacians. On first reading the poem, one sees Phaeacia, or rather Scherie, as the typical fairyland so often found in folk tales. On repeated readings one is not so sure of the glories of Phaeacia. First, it is hard to see how the Phaeacians belong to the Heroic Age despite the superficial resemblance of their society to those of Ithaca, Pylos, and Sparta. For there is no stress, no challenge, in their lives. And there are odd contradictions: they have fine ships and they are famous sailors, but they have nothing to do with other people. They seem to prefer to live in a kind of splendid isolation, a sort of suspended animation where they can avoid contamination with the rest of the world. At the beginning of Book VII there is even a hint of incest in the royal house: the king, we read, is the queen's uncle. And later on, in Book XIII, at the very beginning, when the Phaeacian leaders offer gifts to Odysseus, they assure him they will get back the cost of the gifts by levying a special tax on the people. They are a paradoxical people, and they seem to have developed a special mixture of inbred charm and self-engrossed boorishness. Of course, it is hard to condemn the Phaeacians after their hospitality to Odysseus and their escorting him back to Ithaca, but in the superficial attractiveness of their ways they represent fully as much a peril to Odysseus as do the Cyclopes—who were once their neighbors (VI, 5). The Cyclopes are obviously violent savages; and one way often used to describe the Phaeacians would be to see their gingerbread world as far above the normal level of civilization as the Cyclopes are below it. The Cyclopes may be undercivilized, but the Phaeacians are obviously overcivilized. Their life has no promise, no potentialities, no dynamism; to remain with them would drain Odysseus of his heroism by depriving him of any chance or need for action. It would be a living death.

The illusory quality of life among the Phaeacians and their sinister appeal to Odysseus is reinforced by the fairy-story setting of Nausicaa (who has a genuineness, a touch of life missing from the other Phaeacians), and by Odysseus' performance at the games. Here we have all the ingredients of the conventional tale of the handsome stranger from over the sea who wins the hand of the local princess by overcoming her local suitors in contests of skill and strength. We have seen before how Homer uses techniques, like the Agamemnon motif and the family similes, to rehearse the main action of the poem and to remind us what his poem is about. Since the whole purpose of Odysseus' wanderings is his return to Ithaca, it is well to see how Homer prepares us for Odysseus' arrival at his home. Twice in the poem Odysseus appears in a strange city and each time the method of his arrival foreshadows the climax of the *Odyssey*. The first account was Helen's description in Book IV of how Odysseus infiltrated the city of Troy before its fall. Disguised as a beggar he slipped into Troy and was discovered by Helen who bathed him; and disguised as a beggar he will slip into Ithaca and be discovered by Eurycleia when she bathes him. The conclusion of this tactic is suggested by events now among the Phaeacians which will be repeated in Ithaca in a much grimmer setting. Odysseus arrives in these places, which are both islands, as a stranger; he is insulted by the local youths, here by Euryalus and there by the Suitors; he defeats his ill-mannered competitors in each instance and "wins" the girl.

Another example of Homer's skill in focusing the themes of the *Odyssey* in small and unexpected ways is the Lay of Demodocus or Ballad of Ares and Aphrodite. Ancient critics were offended by this little story on moral grounds and modern critics on linguistic grounds, but it would be high injustice to excise this amusing account of what happened to Ares when he tried to make love to Aphrodite while her husband was out of town, for not only would the *Odyssey* be robbed of one of its funniest interludes but it would also be weakened structurally. For this little anecdote has a kind of languor and irreverence to it that are fully in keeping with the atmosphere of Phaeacia; yet in its account of adultery discovered and deservedly punished, it distills and concentrates the themes of Love and Justice that are central to the *Odyssey*. The tone, of course, is properly frivolous as the gods comment on the spectacle of Ares hung up with Aphrodite in chains of gold; but the events described are, like those of the Agamemnon motif, slanted toward the situation in Ithaca. Ares, the villain in the story, equals Aegisthus, the villain in the Agamemnon myth, and the Suitors, who are the villains in Ithaca; Aphrodite, the goddess of love, is somewhere between the faithful Penelope and the unfaithful (and murderous) Clytemnestra. Hephaistos is deceived, as is Agamemnon, but he punishes the intruder, as does Odysseus. The parallels are not mechanically exact, but in general the scheme holds. And once again what seems ornamental turns out to be functional as Homer uses his literary resourcefulness to preserve thematic direction in a narrative that might otherwise seem rambling and diffuse.

So all in all this experience with the Phaeacians is an important stage in Odysseus' return to Ithaca. It foreshadows the events of his return, and it is at the banquet given him by the Phaeacians that Odysseus tells the story of his previous troubles. Hence the Phaeacian episode recalls Odysseus' past and links it with his future. But the Phaeacians are not merely the means of Odysseus' homecoming: in the temptation offered Odysseus to marry Nausicaa ("It is characteristic of Homer to make his good woman more tempting than any bad woman could be" [9]) and live among them they are a menace to his manhood. Odysseus is a hero; he operates best in danger through cunning and courage. He lives the strenuous life. King Alcinous himself tells us what kind of life the Phaeacian lives. "Though our boxing and wrestling are not beyond criticism, we can run fast and we are first-rate seamen. But the things in which we take a perennial delight are the feast, the lyre, the dance, clean linen in plenty, a hot bath, and our beds" (VIII, 246-49). This is not the stuff of which heroes are made.

In Books IX through XII Odysseus tells the story of his recent past. It is a "tale told through tears" (IX, 13), a motif to be repeated when Aeneas tells his sorrows to Dido and Francesca hers to Dante. The reader of the *Odyssey* is usually surprised here at IX, 19 ("I am Odysseus, Laertes' son"), to realize that up to now the Phaeacians have not learned the identity of their gifted guest. Identity is important in the *Odyssey*, as we have seen, and here, as in Ithaca, it is not disclosed until its impact can be registered.

> When Odysseus comes into the presence of the Phaeacians he at first hides his identity and later shows such wonderful athletic ability that they are interested in him for his own sake. Then the bard repeatedly sings of the glories of Odysseus and his exploits at Troy; hence the athlete's glory won by an unnamed stranger easily merges into that of the hero. It is only by withholding the name of Odysseus that the poet can show in his presence how great was his heroic renown in the land of the Phaeacians, and it was only by the glory he had won as a nameless victor that the Phaeacians could accept without questioning and at once this unknown stranger as the illustrious Odysseus. No audience not aroused to enthusiasm by what Odysseus is and has been would listen for hours to the long story of his wanderings. The real purpose of the games and the songs was to create this enthusiasm.[10]

Book IX is about the Ciconians and the Lotus Eaters in brief and then in more detail about Odysseus' trouble with the Cyclops named Polyphemus. For a Greek audience the Cyclopes were the true savages of the poem because they live alone with "no assemblies for the making of laws, nor any settled customs" (112). But for all their barbarism and their violence, there is something oddly appealing about the Cyclopes, a blend, perhaps, of pastoral and cannibal. Polyphemus whistles when he goes off to tend his flocks, and although he does eat people, he washes them down with milk—and monsters who whistle and drink milk cannot be all bad. Later on, when Odysseus is being carried out the door under a heavy-fleeced lamb, there is something of pathos, of natural compassion, in Polyphemus' speech to his favorite ram:

Sweet ram, what does this mean? Why are you the last of the flock to pass out of the cave, you who have never lagged behind the sheep, you who always step so proudly out and are the first of them to crop the lush shoots of the grass, first to make your way to the flowing stream, and first to turn your head homewards to the sheepfold when the evening falls? Yet to-day you are the last of all. Are you grieved for your master's eye? (447-53).

It may be that the ram is grieving for his master's eye, but Odysseus is not. In fact, the only thing on Odysseus' mind now that he has escaped Polyphemus is to make sure that Polyphemus knows clearly and precisely who it was that drove that stake into his eye. That "My name is Nobody" ploy was fine to help Odysseus escape, but though Greek heroes may exist by their wits they live by their reputations. With a hazy view of the next world, they preferred to think that true immortality was provided by the songs and stories told of what one achieved in this life. So Odysseus now does everything but spell his name. "Cyclops, if anyone ever asks you how you came by your unsightly blindness, tell him your eye was put out by Odysseus, Sacker of Cities, the son of Laertes, who lives in Ithaca" (502-5). We usually think of Odysseus as tricky, cautious, prudent—a hero, to be sure, but the kind of hero who looks twice before he leaps and then leaps a little further, just to make sure. This is true, but more important is his hard egoism, his sense of identity, his pride in being himself and making sure everyone, particularly his defeated enemies, knows it. In the heroic ethic pride is the great virtue, and here Odysseus risks all to exercise it. The result of this self-advertisement is that Polyphemus knows that it is Odysseus who has blinded him, and in retaliation he calls upon his father Poseidon to punish Odysseus. This is the curse that Odysseus suffers under in the remainder of his homeward journey. Poseidon cannot kill Odysseus, because Odysseus is "destined" to arrive home and destiny is somehow larger than the will of the gods, but he can retard and torment Odysseus at his convenience.

In Book X there is another set of three adventures, the first being with Aeolus and his Bag of Winds. There are some questions here, though perhaps not the kind one should direct at a folk tale. Why, for instance, does Aeolus, the King of the Winds, give them away so readily? And why doesn't Odysseus tell his men that he has the winds, and not "a fortune in gold and silver" (35), in the bag? He has nothing to lose by telling them; they are just as anxious as he to get home. The next adventure is with the Laestrygonians, where Odysseus loses all his fleet except his own ship. Here Homer is in disagreement with the beginning of the poem where it is stated that Odysseus lost most of his men on the Island of the Sun. Homer might seem to distinguish between the men on Odysseus' own ship and the men in his fleet, but this is certainly not clear from the context. The next long adventure is with Circe on the island of Aeaea. Circe is the third of the women who tempt Odysseus, as cool and self-possessed as Nausicaa was naïve and impulsive. It is she who turns men into pigs, a bad enough fate by itself, but aggravated by the men's being aware of the transformation: "Their minds were as human as they had been before the change. Indeed, they shed tears in their sties" (240-41). Odysseus is able to counteract Circe's spells with the use of a magic plant called moly. Since a god, Hermes, gives it to him freely and spontaneously, the allegorists have explained it as divine grace, though it is not at all clear how such an interpretation allows for Odysseus' subsequently sleeping with Circe.

The next stage in Odysseus' wandering is foretold to him by Circe, who informs him after a year's sojourn on Aeaea that, "Before I can send you home you must make a journey of a very different kind, and find your way to the Halls of Hades and Persephone the Dread, to consult the soul of Tiresias, the blind Theban prophet" (490-93). Homer here uses a common Greek impersonal verb: the journey *must* be made. Why *must* Odysseus go to the land of the dead? Circe gives him no reason except a kind of necessity, as if this trip to Hades were an appointed stage in his wanderings which he must endure before he can return home. Of course, the ostensible reason for this trip, the so-called *Nekyia,* is that down in Hades Odysseus is to get directions from Tiresias the prophet about how to get home to Ithaca, but we later find out that Tiresias is not much help, for he says not a word about the Sirens or about Scylla and Charybdis. In fact, it is Circe who gives Odysseus this important information—but she was perfectly able to tell him how to get home before she sent him off to the nether regions. And this brings up another peculiarity about this Underworld. It does not seem to be under the world, and Odysseus never reaches "the Halls of Hades and Persephone the Dread" as Circe had directed. Furthermore, when Odysseus does make the journey there in Book XI, this hero, who is so pre-eminently a man of action, has nothing to do. He talks a bit, but mostly he stands still, watches, and listens. As suggested in Chapter II, Odysseus in the Underworld acts much like Telemachus in the *Telemacheia:* both are spectators at an unfamiliar pageant. Telemachus journeys from the tensions of Ithaca, where his mother holds impatient suitors at bay, to the togetherness of Pylos and Sparta, where retired warriors reap the rewards of survival—he passes, as it were, from death to life. By contrast, Odysseus passes from life to death; but the result is that father and son are each in an alien element, where nothing in his previous life prepares either one for his present experience.

Why does Homer have Odysseus make this trip? Odysseus' limited activity in Hades suggests that Homer did not inherit an elaborate mythic tradition from which he could adapt an "adventure" rich in detail or incident. In fact, the scrappy and abrupt quality of Book XI, particularly in its transitions, has led many critics to banish it from the *Odyssey* altogether. This is a possible, though drastic, solution to the problem of the *Nekyia*, and leaves us still to ask how it functions in the poem as it now stands. Did Homer (or whoever) intend this episode to be a radically different kind of experience for Odysseus, a passive absorption of a new wisdom? Or was the purpose of this trip to exalt Odysseus above common humanity as the man who overcame death, who, as Circe remarks admiringly at the beginning of Book XII, has lived twice? We speak of people who have undergone violent or frightening experiences as having "gone through Hell." If Odysseus on his way home must undergo typical perils, must he also have "gone through Hell," have had a vision of a world beyond this world if he is to be properly tested and tempered, fully prepared for the troubles ahead in Ithaca? Is Odysseus' fate meant to be cosmic in its implications? Must he go beyond and beneath the world, penetrate to an unseen source of power, and return vitalized to the trials of traveling and to the culmination of his return—the massacre of the Suitors and his reunion with Penelope? Are the things Odysseus sees in the Underworld meant to invigorate him with an access of vicarious experience? Is the whole trip a kind of rebirth? These are some of the possible questions one can ask about the *Nekyia*, though not without a misgiving that the questions, with their portentous implications, require the kinds of answers that the *Nekyia* is not likely to yield.

Certainly, the idea of passage from life to death and back again is familiar to us from the Bible, where, in the New Testament, Christ often says that man must die if he is to truly live: "He that loseth his life for my sake shall find it" (Matt. 10:39). In St. John's Gospel, the idea of passing into the earth is made explicit: "Except a grain of wheat fall into the ground and die, it abideth alone: but if it die, it bringeth forth much fruit" (John 12:24). And the Trip to the Underworld is a fixture in world mythology and world literature. Among the Greek mythical figures, Theseus, Heracles, and Orpheus all visited the Underworld, and in Christian belief Christ himself descended into hell. In literature there are the obvious instances of Odysseus in *Odyssey* XI, Aeneas in *Aeneid* VI, Dante and Vergil in the first canto of the *Divine Comedy,* and the fainter examples of Achilles in his tent, Hamlet in the graveyard, and Don Quixote in the Cave of Montesinos—each hero temporarily detached from the burden of his obsessions, gathered to a new vision, prepared for a different destiny. The Trip to the Underworld, as early as the *Odyssey,* and before Homer in the *Gilgamesh Epic,* is an archetype, one of those ancient themes, or situations, or images that have recurred in Western literature independently of any literary influence and seem grounded in enduring patterns of the imagination. Perhaps, then, it is pointless to talk of why Odysseus goes to the Underworld, futile to look for motives, reasons, causes. Odysseus goes because all heroes go, because this is an appointed stage in a traditional journey, the roots of which are too deeply buried in primitive ritual to be explainable in terms of rational categories. Homer feels the imperatives of this tradition to be more pressing than the logical requirements of his plot. Circe is right—Odysseus *must* go to the Underworld, even if he finds little to do once he gets there. In fact, to judge from other works of literature, the hero's condition of tenure in the Underworld seems to be passivity, a suspension of his normal activity long enough to allow for some sort of spiritual clarification or insight.

Homer's Book of the Underworld may be divided, roughly, into six sections: first, Elpenor and his request for burial; second, Tiresias and his description of Odysseus' continued wanderings; third, Odysseus' interview with his mother Anticleia; fourth, his meeting with the heroines who suffered for love; fifth, his meeting with the heroes of the Achaean camp at Troy; and sixth, his vision of the suffering sinners. All these are, in an amorphous way, elements of Odysseus' past and future, and the sequence of incidents in Book XI matches the subsequent progress of the poem. Odyssesus first buries Elpenor, then follows Tiresias' advice in his journey home, next meets a member of his family (Telemachus), then sees Penelope, who has suffered for love of him, next performs the heroic deed of warfare, and finally sees the vendetta that has erupted over the Suitors' misdeeds and Odysseus' cruel vengeance settled in an atmosphere of justice. Still, the problems attendant on these encounters are numerous. First, there is that mysterious prediction by Tiresias that Odysseus must make an inland journey after he has returned home.

> You must then set out once more upon your travels. You must take a well-cut oar and go on till you reach a people who know nothing of the sea and never use salt with their food. . . . When you fall in with some other traveller who speaks of the "winnowing-fan" you are

carrying on your shoulder, the time will have come for you to plant
your shapely oar in the earth and offer Lord Poseidon the rich sacri-
fice of a ram, a bull, and a breeding-boar. (XI, 121-31)

This is indeed an obscure set of instructions. Why must Odysseus,
who has just completed his travels, set out again? To propitiate
Poseidon in some inland area where the sea god has no power? But
the purpose of propitiation or appeasement is not made explicit,
and besides, Poseidon will have already had his satisfaction, with
Odysseus arriving home "late and in evil plight." [11] Can Odysseus'
setting up a sea-cult in the midst of dry land celebrate his victory
over the sea? But to become a missionary of Poseidon is an odd sort
of celebration, and where in Greece would an oar not be recog-
nized? After his sea journeys Odysseus was able to find the dry land
of Ithaca; must he now bring the sea to the dry land? One thing is
certain: Odysseus is not home to stay, at least not for the present.
He has done his work in Ithaca, and now he must set out again. One
critic, admiring these mysterious lines, suggests that for Homer, as
for Tolstoy, there are no neat wrap-ups. Life continues in its fa-
miliar patterns and the new is rather like the old—Natasha gets
stouter, Nikolay more narrow-minded.[12]

Odysseus' next interview is with his mother, and a very tender
scene it is too. One or two logical discrepancies here have long
heated the eyes of watchful Analyst critics—that Anticleia, for in-
stance, speaks of Telemachus as full grown and "in peaceful posses-
sion of the royal lands" (184-85), when she had died either when
he was small or else after the Suitors moved in; or that Odysseus
should ask his mother about the condition of Ithaca after Tiresias
had just told him of the suffering in his house. But there is some-
thing very touching, almost sentimental, about a hero who learns
of trouble from as austerely an official source as a prophet and then
turns to his mother with the same question, asking this time not for
information but for the comfort and consolation a son can expect—
and here gets—only from his mother. Anticleia then tells her son
of the agony of separation from Odysseus that made his father a
recluse and sent her to her grave, and this very moving scene ends
with the gesture (to be repeated later by Vergil and Dante) of
Odysseus three times vainly seeking to embrace the shade of his
mother. Anticleia is but one of a number of mythological ladies
who have suffered for love, and Odysseus now sees "all the women
who had been the wives or the daughters of princes" (227).

Here Odysseus' narrative breaks off briefly and we are reminded
that we are in the hall of Alcinous' palace and that we are listening
to a tale told by the guest of honor. This intermezzo separates the

previous group of figures—all women, all of at least a generation before Odysseus, and practically all from Boeotia—from the next, Agamemnon, Achilles, and Ajax—all male, all Odysseus' contemporaries, and all participants with him in the siege of Troy. If everything else in this book were proved to be non-Homeric, these three magnificent interviews would still rank with Homer's most inspired creations. First, Agamemnon gives a vivid account of how he was put to death at the homecoming banquet given for him and his men by Clytemnestra and Aegisthus. As we saw in Chapter I, Homer's picture here of blood spilled over a festive table varies from the more familiar version of Agamemnon's death in the bathtub and makes this deed done to the returning hero more a sacrilege than a crime. At the same time this picture of perverted hospitality reminds us that this is what the Suitors are doing and prefigures the feast Odysseus will give the Suitors before he puts them to death. Agamemnon then speaks of his wife and asks of his son, giving voice to the family concern that is so strong in the *Odyssey*. Odysseus, unable to give Agamemnon information about Orestes, turns next to Achilles. Maynard Mack has called attention to the "two voices" in Western literature, that of the hero and that of his foil. The hero is passionate and purposeful, absolute in his demands, and his characteristic idiom is hyperbole, while his foil is suppler in speech and action, less rigorous, more patient, prepared to compromise, representative less of the values of the individual than of those of the community.

> What matters to the community is obviously accommodation—all those adjustments and resiliences that enable it to survive; whereas what matters to the individual, at least in his heroic mood, is just as obviously integrity—all that enables him to remain an *individual,* one thing not many. The confrontation of these two outlooks is therefore a confrontation of two of our most cherished instincts, the instinct to be resolute, autonomous, free, and the instinct to be "realistic," adaptable, secure.[13]

The two voices of Homeric epic are those of Achilles and Odysseus, and their meetings, whenever we find them in the poems, yield dialogues expressing radically opposed visions of life. When, in *Iliad* XIX, Achilles returns to the battlefield and says that he will not eat ("Food and drink mean nothing to my heart/ but blood does, and slaughter . . ." (213-14), that all he wants is revenge, and Odysseus answers that there is a time to fight and a time to eat and now is the time to eat, we have more than a disagreement over tactics; we have a confrontation of two attitudes that will echo throughout

Western literature ("I would inform you, Sancho, that it is a point of honor with knights-errant to go for a month at a time without eating" [I,10]). Achilles and Odysseus cannot really understand one another, for each operates on a different wave length and at a different intensity. Here in the land of the dead the opposition still obtains, as each attempts to compliment the other and can only compliment himself. Achilles' honor, which Odysseus respectfully salutes, has brought him only death, while Odysseus' survival has been purchased at the price of glory. But these are relics of the past; and Achilles' words are more in keeping with the subject of the *Odyssey* when he worriedly asks about his son and father and when he departs, proud and relieved, after Odysseus has assured him of Neoptolemus' bravery. The final meeting is not really a meeting at all since the proud Ajax stands aloof from Odysseus, and not even the unexpectedness of Odysseus' appearance among the dead can overcome Ajax's resentment at having been cheated of the arms of Achilles (they were awarded to Odysseus after Achilles' death), a humiliation that drove him to suicide. Odysseus has had little satisfaction from winning Achilles' arms and in sympathy and regret he tries to find words, any words, that will assuage the rankling hurt to Ajax's pride. He blames what he can on Zeus, and with some justice, since Zeus' hostility to the Achaeans animates the *Iliad,* but to blame the gods was a tactic much overworked by self-excusing and self-deceiving Greeks, and the ways of the gods meant little to Ajax, the most untheological of Greek heroes. Stanford's description is perfect:

> This is a scene unsurpassed in its sombre pathos—Roman rather than Greek in its majestic austerity. For a moment Ajax wins our admiration like a Cato or a Regulus. For a moment the flexibility of a Ulysses seems cheap and shoddy in the presence of this obdurate heroism. It is the last gesture in Homer of the older heroic style against the newer and more facile fashion. Like some obsolescent creature of the prehistoric world, a solitary mastodon or mammoth faced by a coaxing *homo pithecanthropus* eager to tame its rage, Ajax stalks scornfully and silently away. It is a poor poet who cannot respect a lost cause, who cannot venerate a doomed civilization. As Virgil with all his devotion to imperial Rome did not fail to bring out the pathos of the death of Carthaginian Dido, so Homer here, though his admiration and sympathy in general are for the agile Ulyssean Man, saluted the last of the titanic heroes.[14]

After Odysseus' vain speech to Ajax, the rest of the book is silence. Odysseus is again the observer and his last vision of the Underworld encompasses some famous sinners of myth and legend—Orion, Tityos, Tantalos, and Sisyphus—and, finally, the ghost of Heracles. This is a part of Hades under the supervision of Minos, the legendary king of Crete, and it is probably the one section in the *Odyssey* that not even the most case-hardened Unitarian could defend with much conviction. Analysts point out that the denizens of this part of the Underworld are considerably more active than their counterparts described earlier in the book, and the suggestion that they are being punished here for various misdeeds on earth seems strange in a poem that nowhere else alludes to punishments after death. Of course, the Greeks' notion of the afterlife was always hazy, at best; these sufferings are not precisely punishments since these "sinners" are generally continuing here in Hades what they had previously done on earth; and though it is quite possible for a Sisyphus or a Tityos to continue with his earthly fortunes, it would be much less convenient in the afterlife for the figures of saga to continue in the ways of heroism. But this final section, whether genuine or not, does complete Odysseus' "adventures" in the Underworld in that it provides a moral dimension to his experience that was missing from the earlier tableaux of the book. Orion, Tityos, Tantalus, Sisyphus, and even, though less explicitly, Heracles "sinned" and were "punished." The final lesson of the Underworld is that sinners get punished, and this is also the final lesson of the *Odyssey*. This is the divinely sanctioned assurance with which Odysseus can arm himself when he prepares to face the Suitors.

Book XII brings Odysseus back to Aeaea, where Circe gives him directions on how to get home. (In this respect she is much more helpful than Tiresias.) She tells him about the Sirens, the Drifting Rocks, and Scylla and Charybdis, and particularly warns him against the island of Thrinacia, where the Sun keeps his cattle. Passing the island of the Sirens, Odysseus is, predictably, both cautious and curious, prudent enough to have himself tied to the mast but determined to hear the Siren Song. It is a song worth hearing, with its skillful balancing of identical sounds in the first line (184), "Deur' ag' ion, poluain' Oduseu, mega kudos Achaion" ("Draw near, illustrious Odysseus, flower of Achaean chivalry"), and its special temptation that suggests both the Forbidden Knowledge of Genesis and the occult knowledge of the Faust legend. Odysseus escapes the Sirens, as he does Scylla and Charybdis, but he is not so fortunate with the Cattle of the Sun. His men are beset by hunger—note again the theme of food and hunger—and when Odysseus is away asleep they slaughter the cattle and eat the flesh, although the gods, in a nightmarish scene at XII, 395-96, make it crawl and groan on the spits as they are roasting it. The Sun, Helios, complains to Zeus and Zeus—not Poseidon—destroys Odysseus' ship and all his men. Odysseus barely escapes to Calypso's island, where we first met him in Book V.

In Book XIII we are back in the banquet hall of the Phaeacians, in the palace of Alcinous. The Phaeacians next take Odysseus, asleep, back to Ithaca, for which they will be punished by Poseidon. It is curious that the Phaeacians (in Greek the "dusky men") choose to sail by night, since the Greeks much preferred sea travel by day. Also, Odysseus is brought home asleep, an odd touch at first reading but perhaps appropriate for one now returning from lands of dream and nightmare. For the perils of Books V to XII that Odysseus is now leaving behind him—violence, sensuality, irresponsibility—were somehow not of this daylight world; they were non-heroic (the battle with the Cicones was perfunctory and Odysseus in full armor facing Scylla was a picture of futility), unrelated to the simpler martial virtues that dignified the heroic ideal and achieved glory at Troy. What Odysseus faced during the adventures—overwhelming power and irresistible attractions—was less a challenge to life than a denial of life, and now when he returns home he will awaken to the realities of the Suitors and their campaign for power in Ithaca. His gifts from the Phaeacians are secreted in a cave and behind him are his victories and his losses, in another world almost, with Poseidon's curse that troubled his voyage now sputtering out in a last petulant blow to the hospitable Phaeacians as he turns their ship to stone and plants it forever in their harbor. The Phaeacians decide to give up escorting travelers: wonderland is now closed.

In Ithaca Odysseus meets Athena and together they prepare their strategy, including Odysseus' disguise as a beggar, for the eventual massacre of the Suitors. We are now past the midpoint of the poem, and it detracts not at all from Homer's achievement to suggest a certain slackening of pace in the second half of the *Odyssey*. The poem moves more slowly as Odysseus spins his interminable lies, the action betrays less design or inevitability, and the poet moralizes his preparations for the mass death of the Suitors. One is tempted to speculate that the flaccidness of this part of the poem, up to, say, Book XVIII, is due to a thinness of received material. Perhaps in the story of Odysseus as Homer received it, the hero landed in Ithaca, disguised himself to get into the palace, and there promptly killed the Suitors and rescued his wife. But this was too simple, too crude, too unconsidered for Homer, interested as he is not only in action but in character. So in its place he developed a vast design of revenge with lies, disguises, and elaborate tactics, interesting in its way and important for the psychology of the story, but without the richness of incident that would key the story to a high tension. In short, Homer was doing a certain amount of "making up" in the next few books, and this is not the normal or the most felicitous mode of composition for an oral poet who works best with strongly traditional materials.

But this is pure speculation; perhaps part of Homer's difficulty in plotting the second half of the *Odyssey* was that in rescuing his hero from the perils—and the charms—of the fantastic, he unavoidably landed him among the banalities of the commonplace. After the adventures, the local realities of Ithaca and the pending unpleasantness with the Suitors must have restricted Homer's creativity quite as much as they did Odysseus' ingenuity. His hero's storied curiosity, so variously exploited during the wanderings of Books V to XII, was limited by the familiarities of his homeland, and his vast resourcefulness was reduced to a single concern: a distasteful design of revenge. In the first half of the *Odyssey* unreal dogs guard golden palaces; in the second half a real dog dies in a dungheap. Of such contrasts are the two halves of the *Odyssey* made, but before the second dog, Argo, dies, he wags his tail weakly as he recognizes his master Odysseus. The hero has returned, and it is the Return of the Hero that is the subject of the last books of the poem and, indeed, the real subject of the *Odyssey*.

·§ IV ·§·

THE RETURN OF THE HERO

Book XIII of the *Odyssey* describes the return of Odysseus to Ithaca; Book XVII describes his return, in disguise, to his palace, and the subsequent books describe the events leading to his return to his wife, his marriage bed, and his royal throne. Return is a fact of the *Odyssey*, a structural element in the form of the poem, but the idea of return is more than just an event of mythology, or just a consequence of the Trojan War's being fought across the Ionian sea from mainland Greece. The idea of return as a life-giving process runs deep and strong in all primitive societies, and anthropologists have often noted how totally the lives of primitive peoples are polarized around the return of natural phenomena. The eternal cycles of night and day, winter and summer, birth and death, rise and fall, permeate their lives and shape their imaginations. To secure and celebrate the return of life is often the purpose of their rituals, and the returning god, hero, or king is a feature of their myths. This is also true of Greek religion and Greek mythology, although such was the inventive and transforming power of the Greek imagination that the myths as we read them today in a handbook of Greek mythology show few traces of the ritual impulse that lay behind many of them. Furthermore, Greek mythology is so inclusive, so adaptable, and so secular that it gathered elements of history, geography, legend, folk tale, and primitive science into a collection of stories so various, so fertile, and, above all, so humane that they have been a source of inspiration ever since for writers, artists, and philosophers. Still, it is possible to relate to Homeric epic not only the realities of Greek history and geography (and neither the historians nor the geographers are very satisfied with Homer's excursions into those areas), but also those of Greek religion—which should not be surprising considering Homer's importance in formulating the Greeks' ideas about their gods.

Scholars are generally agreed that before the Greek-speaking peoples came into Greece early in the second millennium, the indigenous population of the mainland and the Minoans on the island of Crete practiced a religion quite different from that of Greece in later centuries. They worshipped not the familiar Olympians described in Homeric epic, with Zeus at their head, but rather a female divinity, a mother goddess. Although she appears variously as vegetation, mountain, or snake goddess (often accompanied by a smaller male god), her basic role seems to be that of a nature deity, but with her protective functions extending to the king and with her temple within his palace, thus connecting her on one hand with the life of nature and on the other with the stability and integrity of the social order. This nature goddess was displaced by the invading Indo-Europeans, who brought with them into Greece at least one deity, Zeus. This chief deity of a victorious people was so established in power and place that in the subsequent religious settlement the female deities of the pre-Hellenic populations were ranged beneath him as wives and daughters. The female divinity whom we know in Homeric epic as Athena was very likely one of these goddesses; because she had enough prestige to resist family subordination to Zeus, she is depicted in myth as being specially born from Zeus' head. In the process of this religious syncretism Athena's character was changed from a nature goddess to a warrior goddess in order to suit the martial inclinations of the Mycenaeans, though she retained her function as the protectress of kings—a role she plays in the *Odyssey*. Thus the religion of the Bronze Age of Greece was an amalgam of Minoan or pre-Hellenic and Mycenaean elements, with the latter predominating and shaping Greek religion into the patriarchy, under Zeus, that Homer depicts, but with many of the goddesses preserving features of their past connection with the process of nature and the life of the seasons. The mythology of the Greeks was also given its distinctively heroic character by the Mycenaeans, whose exploits and ideals were recorded in the legends of the oral tradition and given their final and—very likely—finest expression in the epics of Homer.

The consequences of this Minoan-Mycenaean synthesis of religious allegiances extended into classical times. The legends of the Mycenaeans permeated Greek heroic mythology, and although Homeric epic established the Olympian pantheon as the official religion, popular cults and rituals retained the emotional appeal of pre-Hellenic rites in their emphasis on initiation, purification, and communion. Many of these ritual practices became formalized into so-called "mystery cults," which were particularly popular in the unsettled period before the Persian War, when individuals emancipated from their older ties of clan sought a religious consolation and security (and excitement) that the official Greek religion was ill-prepared to give. The gods of the Homeric poems are humane, civilized, and powerful, but they offer the true believer no opportunity to purify himself of his sins, to be initiated into a community of other true believers, or to anticipate rewards for his true belief in a better world than this one. The mystery cults filled this need by offering their adherents a religious experience that was emotional and irrational, more like the rites of the Near East than the public and secular festivals of the Greek cities. Though all these cults had alleged foreign origins—Dionysus in Phrygia, Orpheus in Thrace, the Pythagoreans in southern Italy, and the Eleusinian mysteries in Crete—their heyday on the Greek mainland was not the result of forcible foreign intrusions or importations, but rather of the crystallization of certain survivals of Minoan-Mycenaean cult practices. They were a kind of religious revivalism, an effort to bring back into contemporary Greek life the ritualism of an earlier age and afford participants a private and personal approach to divinity. The primitive sacramentalism of these rites promised the initiate the prospect of personal union with divinity and the overcoming of mortality. To participate in a mystery rite was to lose one's old life and gain a new life.

The deities and the myths connected with these cults are generally familiar. Euripides, in his *Bacchae*, describes vividly the cult of Dionysus, of how the women, inspired and maddened by the god, leave the city to join in the nocturnal rites that culminate in the dismemberment of the sacrificial victim. Eventually the Dionysiac cults were tamed and institutionalized in the festivals where, at Athens, the dramas were staged, but Dionysus never wholly lost his identity as a fertility god, the god of the wet element in nature[1] who insures the return and growth of vegetation. Orphism was a more complex cult, with a written body of doctrine that enjoined ritual purity on its adherents as a requisite to immortality. The center of Orphic doctrine was their promise of a cycle of rebirths, in which the soul that dies will be purged and reborn after a thousand-year wait. More familiar, of course, is the story of Eurydice, who was bitten by a snake and died as she attempted to escape the attentions of Aristaeus. Orpheus descended into the Underworld with his magic lyre and persuaded Hades to let Eurydice follow him to the upper world. The stipulation Hades made was that Orpheus must not look back until he reached the sunlight and when Orpheus failed to abide by this, he lost Eurydice forever. The myth that corresponded to the Eleusinian mysteries told how Kore (or Persephone) was abducted by Hades and how her mother Demeter sought her in vain for nine days. On the tenth day Demeter came to Eleusis to the house of King Celeus. There she learned from the sun god Helios of Hades' crime and in her anger she refused to return to Olympus, but instead wandered around the earth forbidding the crops to grow and threatening men with starvation. Zeus saw this and sent Iris to plead with Demeter to return, but she was adamant, even when he offered her gifts, until finally she prevailed upon Zeus to send Hermes down to Hades. Hermes won Kore's release, but only on the condition that she henceforth spend a third of each year in the Underworld. Demeter then returned to the gods and once again "all the broad earth flourished with plants and flowers" (*Homeric Hymn to Demeter*, 472-73).

There are obvious similarities of this Demeter story with the myth of Orpheus and Eurydice. Indeed, there seems to have been a whole family of "rape" myths, all hearkening back to Minoan religion and beyond, and all apparently presenting in discursive form the situation of the Goddess of Nature who periodically disappears—hence the "rape"—and reappears, and the male god who is responsible for rescuing her. Perhaps the most striking myths in this area are connected with Theseus, telling of how he penetrated the Labyrinth in Crete, slew the sacrificial bull which had been devouring the Athenian youth, and on his return carried off Ariadne, who seems to have been a Minoan vegetation goddess.[2] Theseus also joined Peirithous in carrying off Helen, who, like Ariadne, was originally a goddess from the Minoan tree cult, and then later tried to kidnap Persephone herself. Helen was subsequently rescued by Castor and Pollux, but that was not to be the end of her troubles, for after her marriage to Menelaus she was to figure in a much more memorable kidnaping.

At this point it would be well to consider more closely the myth of Demeter. If its origins seem clearly pre-Hellenic, its structure and meaning are considerably less so. Only Walter F. Otto seems to have indicated the chief difficulties of the myth,[3] although one important feature, the virtual identity of Demeter and Persephone, had been noted before.[4] Otto first indicates how suspect is the mother-daughter relationship in this myth: "For though every god has his father and mother, there is no other example of so close a relation between mother and daughter."[5] Otto's second point concerns the disappearance of the vegetation:

> Thus the disappearance of the earth's fertility does not at all coincide with the disappearance of the goddess who supposedly personified the grain. In fact, it occurs considerably later, induced by the angry mother's vengeance. The same version prevails in the famous chorus

of Euripides' *Helena* (1301 ff.). Here Demeter, enraged at what has been done to her, withdraws into the mountain wastes and permits nothing to grow on earth, until at last the gods manage to appease her sorrow.[6]

Thus what we seem to have in the account of the *Homeric Hymn to Demeter* is a contamination of two vegetation myths, one which tells of Kore being carried off by Hades and in which she functions independently of Demeter, and another which tells how the corn goddess Demeter, in wrath at the injustice done her (here the Kore myth provides the justification), withdraws from her place among the Olympians and abdicates her responsibilities until her anger is assuaged by Zeus.

What does all this have to do with Homer? Well, when Homer selected portions of the Trojan War legend to transform into his own kind of epic poetry he composed one poem, the *Iliad,* about a hero who loses his girl, withdraws into his tent, and remains aloof from his soldierly responsibilities as the Achaean fortunes fail, even though offered rich and varied gifts to return. He composed his other poem, the *Odyssey,* about a hero who rescues his wife from Suitors and through his heroism restores peace and justice to the land that had suffered so sorely in his absence. Thus one can almost say that the *Homeric Hymn to Demeter* contains in essence both the *Iliad* and the *Odyssey.*[6a]

This does not mean, of course, that the *Iliad* and the *Odyssey* are melodramas of rape and rescue. It does happen in the poems that women are taken and later recovered—Chryses by Agamemnon, Briseis by Agamemnon, Helen by Paris, and Penelope by the Suitors —but these are incidents of plot in poems that have for their main business the dramatization of the legends of the Trojan War and the portrayal of the idealism of the Heroic Age. Whatever Homer has touched he has transformed and humanized, and the spirit of his poetry is far removed from the props of rite and the quirks of myth. When Achilles, in the *Iliad,* questions the whole value of a hero's life bereft of its sustaining honor, or when he tries to define the conditions of his return, he confronts questions that were no part of a foot-stamping rite. Rites are concerned with the return of life, epic poetry with its quality—the pathos of Hector and Andromache, the frivolity of Paris, the tragedy of Priam, the fidelity of Penelope, the naïveté of Nausicaa. But knowledge of the religious background of the Bronze Age shows us that beneath the splendidly human delineations of his poetry, Homer has exploited patterns of action that have an ageless and mysterious appeal. The terms of Homeric epic are masculine and heroic, but the rhythm of the plots tell of withdrawal and return—Achilles to his tent and back, Odysseus to Troy and back. This configuration vibrates beneath these two poems, giving a special vitality to these myths which have been overlaid by history and folk tale. The return of the day, of the spring, of the crops that sustain and the god that redeems is a primary and powerful theme, and to identify it in the Homeric complex helps us to appreciate how Homer can combine the primitive and the sophisticated, the call of the blood and the prayer of the heart. It reminds us of the truth of T. S. Eliot's dictum that "The artist is and should be more primitive, as well as more civilized, than his contemporaries."

This religious background of the Homeric myths also works with the heroic foreground to enlarge and clarify the themes of the poems. It is the purpose of ritual, be it nature rites or the practices of the mystery cults, to secure and reinforce life. The return of nature's life or a rebirth of the life of the spirit are both means by which man seeks to renew life and overcome death. This is also the message of Homer's poetry, as it is of all art: it recalls to us the conditions of our mortality and enables us to endure the perils and to assert the values of human life, and to maintain these values, however fragile, in the face of a hostile universe. When Achilles returns from the solitude and inertia of his tent, he chooses life over death (however violent and fatal the consequences of this choice are in the context of the *Iliad*). He chooses to act, and his action will redeem his love for Patroclus and ensure victory for the Achaeans. And in the final scene of the *Iliad*, when Achilles faces Priam over the dead body of Hector and recognizes that in their mutual loss they are connected by a bond of suffering humanity that transcends the hostilities that have set them at variance, Homer achieves a poetic and spiritual victory over the death that otherwise haunts the pages of the *Iliad*. In the *Odyssey* the final vision of a family reunited, of a land at peace, and of a divine order that sanctions justice and rewards patience is likewise a recovery of life and an assertion of humane values against the destructiveness of Poseidon and Antinous. This is the miracle of Homeric epic, that its themes are one with its action; in the *Iliad* and the *Odyssey* Homer has achieved the ultimate end of all art, perfect fusion of form and content.

This perfection, which may be rightly claimed for the whole poem, is not immediately discernible at the beginning of its second half. In Eumaeus' hut, amid his dogs and pigs, Odysseus whiles away all of Book XIV, some of XV, all of XVI, and a few lines of XVII. There is an obvious sort of suspense here in this confrontation of

Odysseus and Eumaeus, and in Book XVI Odysseus does reveal himself to Telemachus, but the pace of the poem flattens noticeably in these books even though it may be argued that the reader deserves a moment of stillness between Scylla and the Suitors. One may perhaps point out that a certain progression in Odysseus' recovery of his house and throne commences here. After first meeting Eumaeus, the humblest and remotest of his subjects, Odysseus reveals himself successively to his son, his nursemaid, and his wife, on an ascending scale of family intimacy; finally he is reunited with his father, through whom he has inherited his kingship. But the time and space given to the garrulous Eumaeus seem disproportionate, and the whole episode is not marked by any compensating rustic charm.

Yet even if, as suggested at the end of Chapter 2, the inherited resources of folk tale and legend failed Homer after Book XIII, his art did not. Even toward the end of the poem, where Odysseus girds himself for the grim business with the Suitors, Homer employs a consistent symbolic scheme to key and clarify his action. The symbols are the familiar ones of light and darkness, and they operate through Homer's adroit use of fire imagery. Fire is first mentioned at XVIII, 307, when the Suitors set up braziers to supply light for the evening carouse. At first the maidservants take turns tending the fires, then Odysseus volunteers his services, assuring them somewhat ominously: "I shall provide light for the company" (317). The Greek for light, *phaos*, is a charged word here, since it is often used in Homer (*Iliad* VI, 6; XVIII, 102) to mean victory or deliverance. Eurymachus ridicules Odysseus as he stands tending the burning braziers. "It seems to me that the torch-light emanates from the man himself, in fact from that pate of his, innocent as it seems of the slightest vestige of hair" (354-55). There is an evident irony here in Eurymachus' jest that Odysseus is the source of the firelight, as indeed he is—of the fire that purges and destroys as well as the fire that warms and preserves.

This emphasis on fire-tending is strikingly repeated in the opening lines of Book XIX, leaving little doubt, it would seem, that this effect was contrived by the poet. First Telemachus asks that his father's arms be stored away, "where the fire won't get at them" (20). The nurse wonders who will carry a light for Telemachus, a chore undertaken by Athena, who guides them holding a strange golden lamp (XIX, 34; the word *lychnos* for lamp occurs only here in Homer, light elsewhere being provided by torches or braziers). Athena's lamp floods the hall with so radiant a light that Telemachus marvels at how the walls and beams and pillars are il-

lumined, "as though there were a blazing fire" (39). The fire suggests
the presence of divinity to him: "I honestly believe some god from
heaven is in the house" (40). Telemachus goes off by torchlight to
his bedroom while Penelope comes down from her rooms and sits
"in her usual place by the fire" (55). Her maids "raked out the fire
from the braziers onto the floor and heaped them high with fresh
fuel for light and warmth" (63-64). At this point Melantho (the
prefix of whose name, *mela*, means "black" in Greek, and hence has
a fine appropriateness here) warns Odysseus to leave or else get a
torch thrown at him. Perhaps it is also significant that in the lie
Odysseus then tells Penelope he calls himself "Aithon" or "Blazes"
(183). At any rate, fire and light become increasingly identified with
Odysseus, and he turns from the hearth fire to the darkness to hide
the scar that will reveal him (389). After Eurycleia recognizes him
and he hushes her, he turns once again to the fire to get warm
(505-6). Even in his bed, in the next book, he is like a haggis roast-
ing in the blaze of a fire (XX, 25-27). All night the fire burns (123),
and next morning Odysseus is baited once again, this time by
Melanthus (again the "black" prefix).

Just as Odysseus is associated with light and warmth, the Suitors,
in Theoclymenus' surrealistic vision, are wrapped in night (351);
and, a few lines later, the sun for them has disappeared from the
sky beneath an evil mist (356-57). The next mention of fire is in the
last lines of Book XXII, where Odysseus asks Eurycleia to make
him a fire to fumigate the house: "The first thing I want is a fire
in this hall" (481-82). Then when the other women rush joyfully
in to greet Odysseus, they do so "torch in hand" (497). Finally, at
what has sometimes been taken as the end of the *Odyssey*, Eurynome
makes up Odysseus' and Penelope's bed by the light of torches
(XXIII, 290) and then guides them by torchlight to their room.
Fire has been Odysseus' constant companion in these late books,
from the darkness of his abnegation before the insolent Suitors to
the radiance of his reunion with Penelope.

The most obvious effect of the fire imagery in these books is to
lend the action a dramatic chiaroscuro quality, what one critic has
called Homer's "quasi-Rembrandtian predilection for half lights,
for crepuscular and nocturnal effects." [7] The sharp play of light
and dark prepares us for an equally stark scene of pitiless revenge.
On a symbolic level the fire represents the return of life to the
stricken land of Ithaca. It is evening, the weather outside is cold,
and the stage is set for the return of the life-giving hero from what
Yeats calls the "fabulous, formless darkness." Odysseus, the force
of light, returns to oppose the Suitors, who are veiled, as Theocly-

menus sees it, in mist and night. On another level, fire is both type and antitype. The vital fire of Odysseus, generative and preservative, is opposed to the sterile burning of the Suitors' lust for Penelope. The ambivalence of the fire signs the paradox of their positions: the Suitors, who were the heroes in Ithaca, become the scapegoats, Odysseus the opposite. (The same paradox is implicit in the bow which Antinous hoped to string but which was used against him.) Fire brightens, clarifies, reveals; and it is by the light of the hearth fire that Eurycleia recognizes Odysseus. In the simile in Book XXII, 384-89, comparing the dead Suitors to dead fish heaped on a beach, Odysseus is "the bright sun" that ends their lives. And finally, when Odysseus has settled accounts with the Suitors, it is fire he uses to fumigate his palace, to purge it of the spilt blood of the villainous Suitors.

By way of postscript, it seems almost as if Saint Paul were describing the day of the twentieth book of the *Odyssey* when he writes to the Romans (13:11-13):

> And that, knowing the time, that now it is high time to awake out of sleep: for now is our salvation nearer than we believed [Odysseus unexpectedly arrived in Ithaca]. The night is far spent, the day is at hand [the feast day of Apollo the Archer]: let us therefore cast off the works of darkness, and let us put on the armor of light. Let us walk honestly, as in the day [the harmony and order that Odysseus incarnates]; not in rioting and drunkenness, not in chambering and wantonness, not in strife and envying [the typical vices of the Suitors].

Of course, there can be no talk here of direct literary inheritance; but what is evident is a tradition of symbolism, an inherited rhetoric of good and evil.

This complex of fire references, with its implication of the radical opposition between the forces of light and the forces of darkness, leads up to (and beyond) the fateful scene where good and evil face one another at, characteristically, a banquet. The irony of this final banquet, this last supper, should be obvious. The banquet is to be held on the day of Apollo, the god of archery, and whoever can string and draw the bow will win Penelope as his wife. (It is a little vague whether the archery contest is being held on this day because this is the traditional feast day of Apollo the Archer God, or if—and this seems less likely—the holding of this contest makes this day, any day, sacred to Apollo.) The basis for this scene is very old: it is the traditional prenuptial contest. The man who can perform the feat of strength wins the girl, and the situation here, *mutatis mutandis,* recalls the similar setting of the games in Phaeacia. Here the Suitors suppose that one of them will string the bow and that the evening banquet will become a wedding feast for the lucky man. The irony here is that the bow will be strung, but the wedding banquet will turn out to be a funeral feast. This image of the deathly wedding is interesting, and was foreshadowed by Homer as early as the first book. There Athena told Telemachus, "Yes, if only Odysseus, as he then was, could get among these Suitors, there'd be a quick death and a sorry wedding for them all" (265-66). In Book IV Menelaus repeats these words to Telemachus, "By Father Zeus, Athene, and Apollo, that's the Odysseus I should like to see these Suitors meet. A swift death and a sorry wedding there would be for all!" (345-46). In Book XVII, 136-37, Telemachus quotes Menelaus' words to Penelope when he is telling her of his trip to Pylos and Sparta. Shortly thereafter, in the same book, Odysseus himself warns the Suitors, "I hope Antinous will be dead before his wedding day" (476). Next, in Book XXI, 295-304, Antinous mentions another wedding, that of King Peirithous of the Lapiths to Hippodameia, that turned into a bloody riot when an invited guest, a Centaur named Eurytion, tried to abduct the bride. Antinous uses this example to intimidate the disguised Odysseus, whom he accuses of being drunk, but it is he and his fellow Suitors who will be punished, like Eurytion, for trying to steal Odysseus' wife. So what starts out to be a wedding banquet becomes a funeral feast; and after the Suitors have been slaughtered, Homer seals this irony by having Odysseus command that the minstrel "strike up a merry dance-tune for us, loud as his lyre can play, so that if the music is heard outside by anyone passing in the road or by one of our neighbors, they may imagine there is a wedding-feast" (XXIII, 133-36).[8]

The bow that Odysseus strings also extends this irony. The Suitors think that the bow will be their device to win Penelope, the instrument of their success, when actually it becomes the instrument of their destruction. The bow is also very practical for the needs of the situation: a sword would have brought Odysseus too close to the Suitors, and a spear or lance would have been lost after one throw. The bow is also the weapon sacred to Apollo, who is the archer god. It is interesting that Apollo, who is hardly mentioned in the rest of the *Odyssey,* has a particularly fitting role in the final books. The Suitors who are slain at his feast are more than an overt threat to Odysseus' kingdom. They are an infection threatening the life of the state through its ruling family, and it is altogether appropriate that this infection be excised under the auspices of Apollo, who is also the god of health and purifications.

Furthermore, the fact that Odysseus did not take the bow to

Troy with him (where "arrow-fighter" was a term of derision) suggests that this is not a heroic contest and that the Suitors, however dangerous, are not worthy enemies. There is little conventional heroism in the *Odyssey;* Odysseus rarely engages in any fighting reminiscent of the single combats of the *Iliad,* and now his slaughter of the Suitors lies quite outside the contexts of heroism. This is emphasized by the words of his nurse at the end of the battle. "When Eurycleia saw the dead men and that sea of blood her instinct was to raise a yell of triumph at the mighty achievement that confronted her" (XXII, 407-8). But Odysseus restrains her. "I'll have no jubilation here. It is an impious thing to exult over the slain. These men fell victims to the hand of heaven and their own infamy. They paid respect to no one who came near them—good men and bad were all alike to them. And now their insensate wickedness has brought them to this awful end" (411-16). When a hero feels no surge of pride at the defeat of one hundred and eight foes, but chooses instead to assess the morality of their conduct and the equity of their fate with a fine impartiality, then an era has ended. Homeric epic, which began in the *Iliad* with Agamemnon's petulant act of self-assertion, concludes here in the *Odyssey* with Odysseus' pondered act of self-effacement.

Finally, the Suitors die a very vivid and terrible death. In Book XXII Homer uses successive animal similes to describe them as being as frightened as cattle (299), as defenseless as birds (303-4), and as pathetic as dead fish (384-85), while the same similes depict Odysseus first as a gadfly (300), then as a vulture (302), and finally as a fisherman (384), thereby matching the stages of his increase of power over the Suitors from the beginning to the end of the battle.

After the Suitors are slain there are two major scenes left, the reunion with Penelope, and the defeat of the Suitors' relatives. These correspond to what we have been calling the two great themes of the *Odyssey,* love and justice: the love of Odysseus for his wife and family, Odysseus as husband and father; and the justice he deals out to the Suitors, Odysseus as avenger, as a good but powerful and sometimes merciless king. As we have seen, one can hardly characterize Odysseus' love for Penelope as romantic or sentimental. Odysseus wants to get back to his wife because she is part of his home and hearth, part of his very being. There can be no doubt that he loves Penelope very much, but it would certainly be undignified for an Achaean hero to demonstrate too obvious an affection for his wife, particularly to someone like Alcinous or Athena. It is his father and his land that give Odysseus status and substance in heroic society, and these are his overt reasons for wanting to return home, as when he tells Calypso, "I long to reach my home" (V, 220).

But the motive for personal love and affection is still there, so much so that many critics, both ancient and modern, have claimed that the poem ends at line 296 of Book XXIII, when Odysseus goes to bed with Penelope.[9] This line with its odd middle term, "gladly they came to the place [or rite?] of their ancient bed"—the translation depending on how one renders the Greek *thesmon,* a word used only here by Homer—must have deeply impressed these critics, since to take it as the end of the *Odyssey* leaves them with at least one unresolved issue, the debt of blood incurred by Odysseus for having dispatched so many young Ithacans. But their interest in this line does indicate that the sexual union of Odysseus and Penelope was taken seriously by ancient critics, as indeed it was by Athena, who holds back the dawn and lengthens their night of love. Here Homer has selected one detail, one object, and made it the great symbol of this scene of reunion. This is Odysseus' bed. Just before this scene, at line 177, Penelope tests this man Eurycleia claims is her husband—everybody tests everybody else in the suspicious atmosphere of these books; nobody, least of all Penelope, can afford to be deceived—by ordering her to make up Odysseus' bed outside the bedroom. On hearing this Odysseus goes into a rage ("Who, if you please, has moved my bed elsewhere?"—his anger is significant, since Homer's heroes usually do not feel much attachment to *things,* even to their weapons) and reveals that his is a magic bed, for one post of it is the trunk of an olive tree around which the entire bedroom was built.

It is a bed, therefore, that is rooted in the earth, fixed in place, and consecrated to the stability and union of marriage. It is one of the two poles of the *Odyssey,* the other being its opposite, the Sirens' Song of rootlessness and irresponsibility.[10] It also symbolizes Odysseus' emancipation from the adventures of Books V to XII, from his random affairs with the likes of Circe and Calypso, and his conquest of the temptations of the Lotus Eaters and the Sirens. Like Antaeus, the mighty wrestler and giant who was invincible so long as he was in contact with his Mother Earth, the marriage of Odysseus and Penelope has a primal strength—it is secure, fixed in time and place, yet alive, natural, capable of further growth. The choice of the tree is also apt. It is the olive tree—the same kind of tree that Odysseus sought shelter under when he crawled ashore on the land of the Phaeacians at the end of Book IV and the same kind of tree that grew on the shore of Ithaca where Odysseus was landed by the Phaeacians in Book XIII and in the shade of which Athena

and he first plotted the destruction of the Suitors; the stubborn, re-
silient, fruitful olive tree, as much the staple of life in ancient Greece
as it is today in modern Greece. In Greek myth it was this tree that
Athena planted to best Poseidon in their dispute for the Acropolis;
it was this tree which was burned by the Persians when they cap-
tured Athens in 480 but which, on the very next day, put out a
new shoot (Herodotus VIII, 55). Historically the olive tree cele-
brated the victory of democracy over despotism, mythologically the
victory of civic justice over random violence, and poetically, here
in the *Odyssey,* the victory of married love over sterile lust.

Odysseus, then, is the embodiment of love. By being reunited
with Penelope he preserves their relationship as man and wife, and
by preserving his family he remains the loving father. But Odysseus
has also a public role to play; he is, after all, the powerful king of
Ithaca, the ruler who defeats the enemies who would dare to dis-
order his kingdom and subvert his authority—in other words, the
instrument of justice. As such, he follows the lead of Athena, who
at the very end of the poem is finally responsible for the peace that
is established between Odysseus' party and the Suitors' kinsmen. We
have already seen the particularly close relationship, almost inti-
macy, between Odysseus and Athena. Unfortunately for Odysseus,
however, Athena is not always available, even when he needs her
most, and in her presence and absence Homer diagrams her im-
portance for the poem. It is a curious fact, as we noted, that despite
Odysseus' personal magnetism, he does not have her invaluable
services during his wanderings. In Book XIII, 341-42, Athena tries
to excuse herself by saying that she preferred not to anger her uncle
Poseidon, but this does not explain her absence before the Cyclops
incident and it is contradicted by the fact that she did oppose
Poseidon at the Council of the Gods. One explanation offered is
that the Wanderings are made up of folk tales where Olympian di-
vinities ordinarily would not intrude. Another explanation, and one
more appropriate to the *Odyssey,* is that the maritime adventures,
with their intimate appeals to types of human weakness, were
Odysseus' *personal* trials, which he had to endure alone and inde-
pendently. To Athena Homer has given a more civic role to play
—to make sure that Odysseus gets back to his family and kingdom
and punishes the Suitors—while it is up to Odysseus himself to make
his own way through the incidental and intervening dangers. (Hence
it is Hermes, an unimportant divinity in the *Odyssey,* who is sent
to Calypso's isle to effect Odysseus' release, while Athena herself
goes to Ithaca and Telemachus.) Athena, therefore, is less Odysseus'
personal good luck charm than his protectress in his function as

father and king. In the former role, protectress of Odysseus as father of Telemachus, she appears at the beginning of the poem; at the very end of the poem she is again the protectress of Odysseus in his role as king of Ithaca. Of course this entails Athena's preserving Odysseus from personal destruction, but this is only part of her larger, social purpose.

The civic role taken by Athena in the *Odyssey* is also consistent with current theories about Athena's place in the Greek pantheon. It seems very likely that Athena was originally a pre-Greek goddess, perhaps a nature divinity whose protection also embraced king and palace, like the Minoan house goddess. When the Greek-speaking peoples came into Greece early in the second millennium they brought with them, as we saw earlier, a masculine divinity, Zeus, god of the sky and the weather, and in the process of religious evolution and syncretism (i.e. sacred marriages) the pre-Hellenic goddesses were incorporated into the Hellenic system. In this way Athena eventually acquired a martial status reflecting the warlike propensities of the mainland civilization of the Mycenaeans. "This explains the curious circumstance that the Greek divinity of war is a goddess; above all, she protects the citadel and the town and in older times the person of the king." [11] Once a fertility goddess, Athena eventually acquired Olympian status as Zeus' daughter, although the oddness of her birth—she was born from Zeus' brow—suggests her prestige and the difficulty of the compromise by which she became a member of Greece's divine family. In the *Odyssey* there is even one specific example of Athena as tutelary goddess of the Athenian kings. In Book VII, when Athena left Odysseus in Scherie, she "came to Marathon and the broad streets of Athens where she entered the great palace of Erechtheus" (80). But this relic of religious history is less important than her over-all role in the poem as guardian of Ithaca's king and his household, particularly, as in the *Telemacheia*, of his son and successor. It is one of the smaller miracles of Homeric poetry that Homer has transformed this technical relationship into a temperamental affinity. The usual relationship between a Greek and his gods was a rather chilly *quid pro quo* arrangement, but between Athena and Odysseus there is an affection and an understanding that so deeply affects Athena that in Book XIII she herself has to comment on it: "How like you to be so wary! And that is why I cannot desert you in your misfortunes: you are so civilized, so intelligent, so self-possessed" (330-32).

There is no open warfare in the *Odyssey* and hence no opportunity for Athena to function as a goddess of war, although she can still wield a mean aegis if necessary, as when she drives the Suitors in panic in Book XXII. Athena's war role, however, was never construed as violent or bloody—this was left to Ares. Athena was the goddess of defensive warfare, of the battle that saves the city by courage and prudence.[12] Thus Athena in the *Odyssey* not only is the hero's patron saint, but also is interested in his family, in his reputation as a wise ruler (which she emphasizes in the Second Council of the Gods), and in preserving his house. Hence her absence during the Wanderings and her presence everywhere in Ithaca, particularly at the slaying of the Suitors and the pacification of their kinsmen. Her purpose is to restore Odysseus to the throne, end the threat of vendetta, and replace anarchy with justice in Ithaca.

The social conditions which created a wide popular demand for justice appeared early in archaic Greece. Oligarchic despotism, popular enlightenment, and a developing self-consciousness were only a few of the familiar causes that led citizens in the seventh century to question the rightness and inevitability of their lot. In literature justice became a theme, if not an obsession, of Hesiod's *Works and Days*. In religion it produced a daughter for Zeus, Dikê, whose very artificiality testified to the urgency of her creation. In language, it early gave a conceptual coloring to the Greek word *dikê*, which had originally meant "way," but which came to mean "justice." [13] The etymology of *dikê* is by no means certain, but it seems to be cognate with the Sanskrit *diç—dik* meaning "direction" or "indication" and is hence connected with the Greek *deiknumi*, "to show" or "to point out." It is possible to trace the evolution of *dikê* from the concrete "direction" to the abstract "right" or "justice." In an absolute monarchy, such as the several Homeric kings seem to have enjoyed, the word of the ruler is law and his actions become prescriptive for his subjects. Should a dispute arise, it is the king who, with the advice and, usually, consent of the leading men of his society, prescribes what the disputants must do, *directs* them in their actions. Thus what he decides becomes right and not just by its inherent fairness, but by virtue of his authority. Eventually tradition also creates a body of customs that acquire binding force. These are "the way things have always been done," the accepted *directions* guiding activity and controlling conduct.[14] These "ways" are the paths men take in their dealings with one another. The *directions* these paths take have been defined by the judgments of custom or authority. Good judgments are thus seen as "straight," bad as "crooked," because these judgments still retain their root meanings of "ways" or "paths." The passion for justice in the archaic age arose from a dissatisfaction with a kind of justice that was either traditional or authoritative, and in either case arbitrary, and which, being unavailable in any fixed constitution, depended more on personal whim or obsolete forms than on mutually accepted principles of fair dealing. Justice can hardly prevail in a society where the rules of conduct are unknown or undefined.

Homeric poetry seems to have ripened in the midst of this attempt to conceptualize *dikê* and to define the limits of justice. Here the *Odyssey* seems the more relevant; in fact, the problem of *dikê* may have affected the composition of the poem. In the *Iliad,* Homer has a simile showing Zeus punishing men who pronounce vicious judgments and distort the right (XVI, 384-93), and in one of the scenes on Achilles' shield two talents of gold are to be given to the judge in a dispute who spoke the "straightest *dikê*" (XVIII, 508). In the *Odyssey dikê* occurs much more often, generally meaning "way" but often shading off to "right" or "justice." Guthrie has collected and commented on some of the examples.

> The men of Ithaca have forgotten, complains Penelope, during the long absence of Odysseus, what an unusual king he was. "He never did nor said anything unfair among the people, though that is the *dikê* (the usual way) of god-like kings: one man they will hate, and favor another." In the following we may be sure that the meaning intended was the same, though they show how easily the word could slip from signifying no more than what was customary to indicating what was right and just. (Eumaios the swineherd to Odysseus): "What I have to give is little, though gladly given; for that is the *dikê* of (the way with) servants, who live in constant fear when young men are their lords." (The mother of Odysseus, when he tries to embrace her and finds that she is a mere bodiless shade:) "Nay this is the *dikê* of (what happens to) mortals when one of us dies." (Odysseus, in disguise, to Penelope, who has asked him who he is:) "Thou layest upon me fresh grief in addition to that which I already bear: for that is *dikê* (for so it is) when a man is parted from his homeland so long as I now have been." A pleasant example is furnished by the meeting of Odysseus with his old father, whom he finds working in the fields like a common labourer. Odysseus congratulates him on his husbandry but suggests that he does not look like the sort of man who should be doing this work. He should rather be in a position to enjoy his bath and his meal and then go comfortably off to sleep. "For that is the *dikê* of old men." Here the word may indicate a habit or a right. No doubt Odysseus had both in mind and *dikê* can easily mean both together.[15]

Guthrie overlooks one remarkable scene in XIX, 43, where Athena's special lamp, her *lychnos,* radiates through the hall and astonishes Telemachus. Odysseus hushes him, explaining, "The Olympians have ways of their own, and this is an instance" (43). Here Athena is leading Odysseus and Telemachus, guiding them in their work of stowing away the Suitors' weapons, showing them the "way." This is a domestic task befitting a household goddess, yet in the light of this magic lamp we have a glimpse of Aeschylus' Athena, the goddess of justice, in the making. For her function in the *Odyssey* is to restore justice to Ithaca, and this she achieves by showing Odysseus the *way* back to Ithaca, by showing Telemachus the *way* a young prince comports himself in heroic society, and by showing Penelope a *way* to test the Suitors' skill (the archery contest) and prepare their destruction.

This function of Athena as Goddess of Justice becomes clearer in Book XXIV, a book which many critics claim does not even belong to the *Odyssey*. The last book of the poem opens with another trip to the Underworld, the so-called "Second *Nekyia*," this time taken by the recently deceased Suitors. The action of the Second *Nekyia*, like that of the first, is seen from the perspective of Greek heroism, as that quality of life is illuminated by two of its most distinguished exponents, Achilles and Agamemnon. Into this context of true heroism now arrives the ragged band of Suitors whose sordid and unruly lives and ignoble, if deserved, deaths travestied the ideals of the very society they had hoped to usurp and rule by marrying Penelope. In these lines Homer emphasizes the justice of Odysseus' bloody settlement by confronting these wreckers with two genuine heroes. A life soured by disappointment was for Achilles sweetened by the due glory that attended his leaving of it; for Agamemnon the immensity of his position and his achievements was tragically and unjustly requited by a horrid and undeserved death. But for Agamemnon there remained at least the memory of an eminence recognized and ratified by Zeus the Thunderer, while for Achilles, so persistently obsessed by the precarious worth of the heroic life, the Nine Muses conducted all creation in mourning his departed greatness. Achilles had a bitter life and Agamemnon a bitter death, but for both of them there was the memory of greatness. For the Suitors, whose lives denied the simplest demands of justice as much as their deaths affirmed them, there is neither consolation, and deservedly so.

It is interesting, too, that when the Suitors speak to Agamemnon, they seem to have accepted their fate and its justice. Their account of their misfortunes is remarkably dispassionate; they make no attempt to gloss over their own conduct, admitting even at line 161 that they abused and struck the disguised Odysseus. Why, their only distortion of the facts is to give Penelope's web trick a climactic importance it really did not have and to compliment Odysseus by involving the old schemer in the archery contest device, when in fact this was Penelope's plan, at Athena's instigation. The Suitors' spokesman, Amphimedon, can also afford to be objective, not having been compromised in the course of the poem. All in all, the Suitors show no bitterness, no rage, no resentment. Later on their kinsmen will take up the cudgels for them, but here the Suitors neither ask for any revenge nor do they reckon on any vendetta. If the burden of Homer's song in this book is the reestablishment of justice among both the victors and the vanquished, then the attitude of the Suitors fits perfectly into the poet's design.

But the Suitors' acceptance of their fate lays no constraint on their relatives back in Ithaca who are preparing to avenge their fallen sons and brothers. This kind of vengeance, however, would only breed further revenge and would raise the sorry prospect of a continuing vendetta, as a result of which the suppression of the Suitors' anarchy, so ably managed by Athena, would be undone and Ithaca would be plunged into civil war. But here Athena acts, and when at line 526 Odysseus and his men attack the Suitors' kinsmen, Athena raises a great shout, so great that she overwhelms both sides and stops the fighting. The Ithacans scatter and Odysseus pounces on this advantage, but he is checked by Zeus' thunderbolt and Athena's appeal on the last page of the poem: "Ithacans, stop this disastrous fight" (543). The poem then ends with Homer's relating how Athena established peace between the two factions, thus presiding over the establishment of a new order of justice and peace in Ithaca—just as she would later do for Athens at the end of Aeschylus' *Oresteia*.

This covenant made by Athena pleases Odysseus and gives Zeus no offense: it achieves a total framework of justice. The eventual connection of Athena with justice was inevitable, for she was already goddess of power and wisdom, and what else is justice but power wisely disposed and disposing? Throughout the poem Athena embodies both meanings of *dikê:* she is guide for the king and his family, and symbol of that which makes Odysseus' journey necessary —the harmony she produces in the closing lines of the poem. This harmony guaranteed by a just king had been her purpose throughout the poem, for already in the Second Council of the Gods at the beginning of Book V she had told Zeus and the other gods, "I have come to the conclusion that kindness, generosity, and justice should no longer be the aim of any man who wields a royal sceptre—in fact that he might just as well devote his days to tyranny and lawless deeds. Look at Odysseus, that admirable king! To-day, not one of the people he once ruled like a loving father gives him a single thought" (V, 8-11). Athena's speech here has been attacked (see above, p. 49) as a clumsy repetition of part of Mentor's speech in Ithaca in Book II, 230-41. But it is the way of Homeric epic that men's concerns become the concerns of the gods (often, as in the *Iliad*, to their evident displeasure), and when Athena speaks out among the gods in the words of an Ithacan citizen who is appalled by the depredations of the Suitors and the inaction of Ithacan citizenry, she is giving divine ratification and urgency to the dilemma of king and people that is so important to the *Odyssey*.

Thus Book XXIV is necessary to the poem, for it completes the second great abstract theme of the poem, justice. After the reuniting of Penelope and Odysseus (XXIII, 296), the love theme loses its pressure, being extended now only to Odysseus' meeting his father (where even Laertes' first words to Odysseus show less affection at being reunited with a long-lost son than satisfaction that divine justice has been meted out to the Suitors). The significance of the last book is no longer personal, but civic; its outcome is of great weight and consequence for the future of Ithaca as a happy, peaceful, and well ordered kingdom.

⋘ V ⋙

COMPARATIVE EPIC

It is well nigh impossible in any consideration of the *Odyssey* to treat that poem in isolation. It may be true, as one critic has put it, "that the *Odyssey* shows no awareness of the existence of the *Iliad*," [1] but even if the author of the *Odyssey* knew nothing of the story of the *Iliad* (which seems unlikely), we as readers do not share this unawareness. It is important and inevitable, then, that one deal with the only—and perhaps the best—other available document that can clarify the ways of Homeric poetry. No examination of Greek epic poetry can afford to neglect half the evidence.

The differences between the *Iliad* and the *Odyssey* are as obvious as—and, in large measure, the consequence of—the differences in their heroes. The *Odyssey* has always been more popular than the *Iliad,* perhaps because its plot more nearly renders the usual features of mythology in a context of human interest. The "myth" of the *Odyssey* presents a hero who journeys, who has a number of adventures with adversaries both terrible and beautiful, who visits the land of the dead, and who then comes to a land where he wins a bridal contest, marries the beautiful woman who is the prize, and lives on as king of the country. It is a story of absence and return, of trial and success, and its roots lie deep in the ritual experience that is probably the source of all myth. As secularized by Homer in the *Odyssey* it links the archetypes of myth with the conventions of fiction. The hero is a veteran who has been around; he has a family he has not seen in twenty years; there is a princess in the story, but the woman he wins is his own wife and the rivals he defeats are young bloods who have dared, in his absence, to tempt and insult his wife. Why, he even has a teenage son, gawky but well meaning, and a faithful hound dog. The *Odyssey* thus exploits both the classic pattern of the hero's progress to kingship and the emotive force of a man's love of his home and family. Furthermore, it is a comic poem, its subject (to use Maynard Mack's categories[2]) is life-as-spectacle, and the reader of the *Odyssey,* diverted by the variety of

86

its incidents and the buoyancy of its hero, observes Odysseus from without; whereas the tragic *Iliad* presents life-as-experience, and the reader who would respond to its tragedy must identify with Achilles and share his choices, must be conscious not, as in the *Odyssey,* of the plot of the poem but of the plight of its hero.

And even apart from Achilles the *Iliad* is a harsh and demanding poem. It is a story of war—war which, even when waged under the terms of the heroic conventions, makes men suffer and die. And when war is not cruel it is monotonous, though Homer can redeem the cruelty of warriors by their humanity and can even diversify the monotonous carnage of the middle books of fighting. But the proper locale of the *Iliad* is not the plains before Troy as much as it is the soul of Achilles, and Achilles is not a simple or engaging character. The demands he makes upon the reader of the *Iliad* are almost as imperious as those he makes upon life itself. He is proud, sensitive, intransigent, and he asks for respect; in his scorn for compromise he can repel a modern reader conditioned to admire the compliance and accommodation that Achilles rejects. The *Iliad* also has a more complex and pervasive involvement with the gods, and to the extent that a modern reader may find that the gods needlessly complicate human action, the *Iliad* is less satisfying than the "ethical" *Odyssey* with its simpler scheme of divine justice. Finally, in the *Iliad* Homer deploys a host of characters in an action, the siege of Troy, that is historically verifiable, and this raises historical questions which are absent from the blithely imaginative world of the *Odyssey.*

Despite these differences and divergences, however, the *Iliad* is still underlaid by somewhat the same pattern that we saw informing the *Odyssey*—withdrawal and return, defeat and victory. There is even a rudimentary resemblance between the backgrounds of the two heroes. Achilles was early deserted by his mother Thetis and sent by his father Peleus to Mount Pelion to be reared by Cheiron the Centaur. There he was taught the arts of manhood and, when only six years old, he killed his first boar—one recalls Odysseus' boar hunt on Mt. Parnassus (XIX, 392-466). There are similar stories told, too, about the recruitment of Odysseus and Achilles for service at Troy. Both had been forewarned (in Achilles' case the warning came to Thetis) that the expedition to Troy would be dangerous and both were haled off to Troy only through the trickery of the recruiting officers. These stories are not mentioned by Homer, but they do hint at certain parallels in the past experience of the two heroes and suggest analogous roles in the poems. More important, both heroes are isolated—Achilles certainly more than Odysseus, who appears, characteristically, with wife, son, father, and people in the final vision of the poem. Yet for all Achilles' inaccessibility, the intensity of his friendship for Patroclus surpasses Odysseus' more conventional regard for his men or attachment to his family and homeland. The worlds in which these two heroes move are not the same, but both the remoteness of Odysseus' ten years of travels and the familiarity of ten years on the Trojan plains are marked by the menace they represent to the ordinary courses of human life. Even back at Ithaca the situation is not much better than before Troy: years of loneliness and frustration, present leadership uncertain, the worst elements heartened and determined, the prospect of ruin. All this is as true of the Achaean camp at Troy as it is of Odysseus' beleaguered family in Ithaca, and if there is any doubt of Achaean desperation in this bleak situation, then it is removed by Apollo's plague. This is the setting, identical in the two poems: the lonely hero, the imperilled land, and finally the epic purpose. In each poem the purpose is to rescue the captive woman, Helen from the Trojans, Penelope from the Suitors, and to work the appropriate revenge on her captors. (It is an interesting parallel that the heroines have a sometimes ambivalent attitude toward their captors, Helen infatu- ated with Paris, Penelope at least diverted by the ardor of the Suitors.) The success of this project depends upon one condition, the return of the hero, Achilles from his tent, Odysseus from his journeys through this world and the next.

The way Homer develops his stories in the course of the two poems also reveals a certain parallelism. In Book I of the *Iliad* he introduces the specific action, the wrath of Achilles, that will domi- nate the first half of the epic. Likewise, in *Odyssey* I we hear of Odysseus' absence and this circumstance will determine the action until Book XIII. Both heroes, Achilles and Odysseus, need help and both are assisted by Zeus in the Councils of the Gods. In the *Iliad* Zeus accedes to Thetis' request to honor Achilles and in the *Odyssey* he accedes to Athena's request to help Odysseus. In each book a powerful and resentful deity is not privy to this decision, Hera in the *Iliad* and Poseidon in the *Odyssey*. But in each book the hero has the assistance of a divinity who is personally involved in her charge's welfare. This would be only natural in the case of Thetis, who, besides being a Nereid, a minor goddess, is Achilles' mother, but Homer has certainly sharpened the pathos of the suffering mother who, in some versions of the myth, first tried to murder her son and then deserted him.[3] Similarly, he has heightened the ex- traordinary tie between Odysseus and Athena.

In the second book of each poem there is a debate, and in each book this debate broadens the situation of the opening book. In *Iliad* II we see how Achilles' decision to withdraw from the battle has affected Agamemnon and the Achaean camp. The discussion that ensues after Agamemnon's trial gives epic background, as the old arguments originally justifying the expedition now have to be repeated. The Catalogue of Ships then gives the poem geographic range and inclusiveness. In *Odyssey* II there is also a debate, which extends the implications of Book I by showing that the Suitors, who were boisterous young men in the first book, are actually a serious danger as we see them disregard omens, insult Telemachus, and threaten Odysseus, should he return, with death. The setting of Book I is also broadened to a public assembly in Book II as Telemachus, Halitherses, and Mentor join in a futile attempt to enlist popular sympathy for Odysseus' family.

If *Iliad* II and the Catalogue of Ships connect the angry Achilles with the larger subject of the Trojan War, then *Odyssey* III and IV, though specifically devoted to Telemachus, connect Odysseus' story with the epic tradition. Telemachus' journey to Pylos and Sparta shows that the Greek heroic world involved in the Trojan War extended beyond Ithaca. And the speeches by Nestor and Menelaus are the only opportunity Homer has in the first half of the poem (apart from Demodocus' brief account of the Trojan Horse in VIII) to recall Odysseus at Troy, to remind us of his traditional acumen, and to assure us that his feats in the realm of the fantastic are merely a new and perhaps even minor application of a genius that had its great historical expression at Troy in typical ways: the daring and resourceful Odysseus as disguised spy ferreting out Trojan defenses (IV, 244-50); the fierce Odysseus killing Trojans with his long sword (IV, 257); the prudent and restrained Odysseus checking his impetuous fellow Achaeans within the Wooden Horse (IV, 284); the pious Odysseus championed by Athena (II, 218-20).

In each epic there now intervenes a series of books that form a separate group. In the *Iliad,* from III to VIII, we are in the normal course of the war and, apart from the inconvenience of Achilles' departure, the Achaeans do not advert to his absence. Likewise, in *Odyssey* V to XIII Zeus' plan to return Odysseus to Ithaca is suspended as the poem flashes back to the departure from Troy and Homer puts Odysseus through the marvelous books of his wanderings. Then there comes, in each poem, shortly before the midpoint, a book in which the hero undergoes a crucial experience. These are *Iliad* IX and *Odyssey* XI, both "detachable" books in that they can be excised from the epic without marring the movement of the plot, though their loss would diminish our understanding of the poems. In each book the hero is confronted with the larger implications of his position, and in each book the hero's own activity is limited. The simplicity of Ajax' speech to Achilles reminds us of Ajax' silent reaction to Odysseus' greeting in the Underworld. Ajax has no temperament for dealing with Achilles or with Odysseus, no standards to judge them by, no words to communicate with them. Odysseus promises Achilles what will be his if he returns to the Achaeans (IX, 260-306), Tiresias tells Odysseus what he has to expect when he returns home (XI, 115-20). Phoinix evokes memories of Achilles' family, as Anticleia does for Odysseus. The semi-abstract parable of Ruin and Prayers and the tale of the Kouretes and the Aetolians recall the sinners of XI and the gallery of the ill-fated heroines. Although these are superficial parallels, what is far more significant about these two books is that they interrupt the preoccupations of their heroes, rid them briefly of their self-absorption, and force them to consider the meaning of their actions, in fact of their whole existences. In *Odyssey* XI Odysseus is suddenly in a situation where all his traditional gifts are useless, where the conventional heroic stance is inappropriate, and where the prestige of the heroic assemblage puts even Odysseus off his stride. Odysseus now seems somewhat less commanding a personality when he stands alone and uncertain amidst the heroic departed. And yet if Odysseus is overshadowed, the burdens he must prepare to assume are highlighted in the abstract categories of morality, family, and courage into which these interviews are resolved. Achilles, too, hears from the delegates what consequences his decision has entailed for the Achaean army. He is reminded of his family, of the wider contexts of his heroism, and of the mythic precedents for his situation. Then, in his great speech (IX, 308-429), Achilles is forced to explain, to find words, however inadequate, for his resentment, and to justify himself, however raggedly, not only to the delegation visiting him, but also to us and to himself.

From *Iliad* X through XVIII Homer tells the stories of the battles that rage on between the Achaeans and the Trojans. These are the famous "middle books" where the reader experiences the depth and the weight—and the monotony, too—of the suffering that war inflicts on both leaders and followers. Except for a brief appearance at XI, 598, Achilles is out of sight until the end of this section, apart in his tent, "sulking" (to use the word Gilbert Murray properly called horrid), observing the desperation of the Achaeans as their best men become disabled, aware that their ships are being fired, but relenting only enough to let Patroclus briefly beat back the Trojans until he too is slain. The sameness of these books is matched—on a much lower level—by the sameness of the middle books of the *Odyssey* as the disguised Odysseus makes his way, tediously, from Eumaeus' hut to the royal palace. In both poems Homer is setting the stage for two intensely dramatic scenes, Achilles' return to the battle to avenge Patroclus, and Odysseus' revelation before the astonished Suitors. This is, for Homeric epic, the Return of the Hero; on the formal level, it is what the poems are about.

Once the hero has returned, his presence must be felt. We have already seen how events in the *Odyssey* must be individualized by its hero. Odysseus cannot be content with crippling and escaping Polyphemus; it must be a personalized victory. Odysseus' individuality, the force of his arrival, is hammered home by a series of tests and signs. The action does not mount, relentlessly, to one overwhelming recognition scene. Instead, it lingers tantalizingly over a number of scenes, with Irus, with Argos, and with Eurycleia, each of which might (and in some versions of the myth probably did) serve to make known his presence to the Ithacans. On Odysseus' part, he is all the more Odysseus because he is not a Cretan murderer or outcast or aged beggar—hence the reason for the weary length of his lies and disguises in these middle books. Odysseus is almost masochistic, too, in his acceptance of ill-treatment from the Suitors, but all because this self-abasement will ultimately sweeten his revenge by substantiating and intensifying the effect of his presence in Ithaca. This is Athena's purpose too, and she gives Odysseus no respite. Already in Book XIII, when Odysseus first landed in Ithaca, Athena warned him that he would have to suffer at the hands of the Suitors. "Tell not a single person in the place, man or woman, that you are back from your wanderings; but endure all vexations in silence and submit yourself to the indignities that will be put upon you" (307-10). Then in Book XVII, "Athena appeared before Odysseus and urged him to go round collecting scraps from the Suitors and learning to distinguish the good from the bad, though this did not mean that in the end she was to save a single one from destruction" (360-64). As Homer admits, the purpose of Athena's advice is not to separate the good from the bad among the Suitors, but to expose Odysseus to the wrath of the Suitors. In this scene, Antinous becomes so enraged that he first berates Odysseus and then throws a stool at him. Next, in Book XVIII when Odysseus is being mocked by the Suitors as he stands by the fire, Homer tells us that "Athena meanwhile had no intention of allowing the insolent Suitors to abandon their offensive ways; she wished the anguish to bite deeper yet into Odysseus' royal heart" (346-48). These last words are repeated in Book XX, 284-86, when the hungry Odysseus gets something to eat in peace from the servingmen. Again Athena wants her protégé to suffer, and this time Ctesippus obliges her by throwing a cow's hoof at Odysseus. Later, in the great battle in the hall, Athena appears disguised as Mentor, but instead of aiding the hard-pressed Odysseus she changes herself into a swallow and flies off to perch on a ceiling beam because she wants to continue "to put the strength and courage of both Odysseus and his noble son on trial" (236-37). Of course, some of this harassment that Athena so persistently encourages is intended by Homer to denigrate the Suitors and justify their mass murder, but it also reacts upon Odysseus, forcing him to the limits of his famed endurance and guaranteeing that the Suitors' defeat will be utterly and conclusively his own heroic triumph. Again, to make his return to Penelope seem worth all his efforts, to make her seem intensely desirable, a goal worthy of a hero, Homer works in the passage (XVIII, 160-63) of her change and dazzling appearance before the Suitors. "It was now that Athene, goddess of the flashing eyes, put it into the wise head of Icarius' daughter Penelope to appear before the Suitors, with the idea of fanning their ardour to fever heat and enhancing her value to her husband and her son." The radiance of Penelope's appearance also reflects on Odysseus, brightening his heroism and justifying even the protracted sufferings and weary years of his return.

These extended scenes with the Suitors, which so many readers find (with some justification) tedious, are Homer's way of supercharging the return of the hero Odysseus. They are worth consideration on their own merits, but also because they have a counterpart in the *Iliad*, where the returning hero, for all his impatience, is as slow to face his adversary as Odysseus is to engage the Suitors. The Achilles who emerges at the end of Book XIX has an electrifying presence. Part of Achilles' own humanity died with Patroclus, who was wearing his armor, and now he is done with mortality. He is armed by Hephaistos, fed by Athena, prophesied to by Xanthos; he is a demon in battle, fighting "like something more than a mortal" (XX, 493); he is involved with the very elements themselves when Hephaistos, here symbolizing the heat of his sword (XX, 476) and recalling the fire (XX, 490) of his attack, sends flames against the whirling waters of the Xanthos. Homer superbly communicates the initial impact of his appearance in XVIII, 202-29, through significant details. First there is the blaze of fire from Achilles' head; recall the flame reflecting its flicker off Odysseus' bald pate, a contrast that neatly differentiates the *Iliad* and the

Odyssey in tone and manner. Next there is Achilles' standing apart from the other Achaeans; recall Odysseus' isolation among the Suitors. Then there is the triple blast of his great cry; recall Zeus' approving clap of thunder when Odysseus strings his bow at XXI, 413. Finally, there is the protective presence of Pallas Athena sealing his return; recall her appearance in the form of Mentor at a critical juncture, XXII, 205, in Odysseus' final set-to with the Suitors. Fire, noise, divinity—all the appropriate properties to celebrate the return of the hero. The scene explodes with heroic presence.

In each poem the moment of the hero's return, his revelation in power and glory, is preceded by his mortification and followed by his triumph over his foes and the ensuing jubilation.[4] The mortification of Odysseus is more extended, beginning with his being forced to plot his campaign in a swineherd's hut and pursue it disguised as an aged beggar, but it is best rendered by the spectacle of the king of Ithaca, hungry and abused, the sport of one hundred and eight Suitors. In the battle he then kills the Suitors and purges his palace (even using sulphur) and Ithaca of their menace. Success stories of all ages should end with weddings, and the *Odyssey* is no exception, though Odysseus is already married to Penelope and the wedding celebration is feigned, a bitterly ironic ruse to deceive the Suitors' kinsmen. The general rejoicing must wait until the end of Book XXIV.

Somewhat the same pattern is discernible in the *Iliad*, though once again all "patterns" must subserve Homer's immediate narrative interests. But one of the most moving scenes in all of Homeric epic is a scene of mortification, when Achilles befouls himself in the dust at the crushing news of Patroclus' death as he tries to identify himself with his dead friend. This mortification is extended to Achilles' refusal of food—as Odysseus was refused food. Achilles, like Odysseus, is then successful in his battle as he kills Hector, thereby sating his personal lust for vengeance and incidentally aiding the Achaeans by defeating the best of Troy's defenders. Things are too grimly tragic in the last books of the *Iliad* for the jubilation of victory, because the true victory of the *Iliad* is spiritual, not physical, won by Achilles not over Hector but over himself. Achilles first gave up Briseis, then he gave up Patroclus, and now he is asked by old Priam to give up Hector's dead body. When he raises up old Priam and accedes to his request he is renewing his life and celebrating his return from inaction and solitude by a gesture of pity and compassion. Across the dead body of Hector Achilles looks at Priam and discovers that the ties of humanity that bind them are stronger than the temporary hostilities that separate them, and in the clairvoyance of this discovery Achilles triumphs over the loss, the shame, and the suffering that had made him despair of life itself.

It may seem like a sin against Homer and the light to lump Hector with the Suitors as the "villains" of their respective epics, since the attractiveness of Hector is one of Homer's finest achievements. Yet both Hector and the Suitors are the crucial, if not the final, obstacles to the heroes' success, and though Hector is one and the Suitors are one hundred and eight, still the analogy persists.[5] First, the death of Hector is not isolated, but is preceded by Achilles' slaughter of the Trojan rank and file and is then extended and aggravated by the cruel desecration of his body. And at Patroclus' funeral Achilles slaughters another twelve Trojans. On the other hand, the Suitors are many, but few of them are individualized, and in fact so great and unwieldy is their number that they impress one as a single force. In each poem, however, the attitude of the hero is appropriate: Achilles' fury, which overwhelms and obliterates Hector, and Odysseus' dispassionate cold-bloodedness, which dispatches the Suitors without any sense of heroism or cry of triumph. Then, typically, where Achilles cuts his way through to Hector, Odysseus' confrontation of the Suitors is carefully planned and deftly staged. Finally, both Hector and the Suitors deny the ideal of personal, assertive heroism that informs Homeric epic and is the dynamic force in the characters of Achilles and Odysseus. Theirs is the way of collectivism—Hector is trapped in a situation he never made and pressured into action by his family and his city, the faceless Suitors' mass revolt is vague in purpose and unsure of its own strategy. Both parties lack the hard egoism that is the *ultima ratio* of individual *aretê* and substitute for it the obligations of community and class.[6] Hence their threat extends beyond the specific action of the poems; it undermines the hero's reason for being by offering other possibilities, alternative ideals of personal activity. Of course, Hector is still a hero, concerned with his reputation, and the Suitors want one of their number to be king, but in their reactions to the heroes they portend a time when the mystique of heroism, proud and predatory, will be outmoded and men will seek their ideals in more inclusive modes of social behavior.

The Antinous-Hector connection can also be applied to Poseidon and Agamemnon, the other two "villains" of Homeric epic. It is interesting that both Poseidon and Agamemnon darken only the first halves of their respective poems, with the former's malefactions ceasing after Odysseus gets ashore in Ithaca in Book XIII and the latter admitting his folly by IX, 115. If Hector and the Suitors threatened the heroes from non-heroic positions, Agamemnon and Poseidon threatened them by an excess of the arbitrary power that was both the glory and the burden of the heroic code. In insulting Achilles by taking away Briseis, Agamemnon committed a nakedly gratuitous act of self-assertion that undercut the mutual respect that stabilized heroic society. Poseidon exerted his divine power in the service of a curse, and from this position of primitive advantage tried to make Odysseus' wanderings as painful as possible and thereby force him to despair of the life he loved and the family he longed for. Both Agamemnon and Poseidon forced the heroes to justify their *aretê* by confronting its denials: Achilles when he gropes in IX, 308-429, to isolate and define the absolutes of heroism; Odysseus in his plugging persistence to stay alive, keep going, cut his losses, and get home. Both Achilles and Odysseus will soon enough confront their specific enemies, and when they do, in the second half of their poems, each shows how he has survived the generalized menace of the first half. The pent-up violence of the pent-up Achilles explodes in Hector's face, and all the resourcefulness, wile, and sheer bravery that brought Odysseus home is turned on the Suitors. It is no wonder that Hector cuts and runs or that one hundred and eight Suitors are no match for one hero. Achilles has humbled Agamemnon, Odysseus has outlasted Poseidon, and if both heroes seem excessively bloodthirsty in dispatching their final foes, it is because they have been through hard schools and taught by cruel masters.

Minor details serve to extend this over-all parallel to the end of the *Iliad* and the *Odyssey*.

> The climaxes of the two poems show many similarities: in both cases the peripeteia occurs in the antepenultimate episode (or the twenty-second book) of the poem; the events of the day of the climax are most fully described; the psychological state of the hero is pictured before the day begins; most of the characters, including the gods in the *Iliad*, and Athena, the only divinity concerned, in the *Odyssey*, are massed on the stage for the dénouement, and the heroines, Andromache and Penelope, are removed from the scene until the issue is decided. . . . In the conclusions of the two poems the stage is crowded, and in both poems there is a balance between opening and closing scenes.[7]

Each poem has a penultimate ending: *Iliad* XXII, where the revenge story concludes with the death of Hector, and *Odyssey* XXIII, the climactic scene of the love story of Odysseus and Penelope. But to end there would be discordant, and the remaining lines of each poem restore a sense of harmony, of normalcy. For the *Iliad*, with its personal bias, it is a sense of kinship deepened by suffering; for the *Odyssey*, social in intent, it is a promise of peace with justice. Hermes also appears at the end of each poem, and in his capacity as guide he conducts the defeated Suitors to the land of the dead and the defeated Priam to the slayer of his son.

The aim of this chapter's analysis has been to identify the basic structural element in Homeric epic—the pattern of action surrounding a returning hero—and to separate it from the infinite riches of Homer's other achievements. The cycle of withdrawal and return is a basic one in the processes of life and its appeal is primal and instinctive. What Homer gives us in his poetry is the story of the return of the hero to the people who need him so sorely, whether from Troy to Ithaca via the land of the dead, or from a tent to a battlefield via the tragic transcendance of slighted honor. The reactions to experience in Homeric epic are various: Achilles rejects the world, Odysseus accepts it, Telemachus is initiated into it, Laertes has retired from it. Each, in time, returns to the contaminations of commitment, confronts his responsibilities, accepts his burden, and rescues himself and his land. This means that the Homeric focus is dual, at once on the lonely hero and again on his abandoned people.

Here Homer accommodates his art to the fullness of his materials. The "hero line" of the *Iliad*, marked by Achilles, is suspended for much of the poem while the hero is off in his tent. In this void Homer can exploit the richness of the individual fortunes among the Achaeans and Trojans in the great battles of Books III to VIII and X to XVII. This is Homer's "other line," and here the opportunities are unmatched since his heroes are many, their personalities diverse, and their situation critical. In the *Odyssey* this "other line" is not nearly so promising. Penelope's one gambit, the funeral shroud for Laertes, has been played, and her opposition to the Suitors has reached an irritating stalemate. Homer has little to exploit in this impasse and so he uses the *Telemacheia* to take up the slack, but even here he reproduces a heroic theme, though in a minor key. But for him the *Odyssey*'s "hero line"—i.e., the absence of Odysseus—is pure potentiality, and here he works in the array of adventures in Books V to XII, whether (in descending order of likelihood) using traditional Odyssean tales, modifying sea *Märchen*, or freely improvising, is probably impossible to say. The fascination of these exotic adventures is perennial, and the Siren

Song and the Lotos Eaters have become part of Western man's psychological vocabulary.

For Achilles, off in his tent, there is a solitude broken only by an occasional song of the deeds of heroes—art substituting for life. Withdrawn, he has no trials as such, no monsters to slay, or storms to survive. His suffering is infinitely more exquisite, for it is compounded of his own wounded pride, Agamemnon's arrogance, and the Achaeans' suffering. It is the frustration of memory and desire, of heroic *aretê* curdling in isolation, its prior achievements unrewarded, its current opportunities unrealized. The monster Achilles continually duels is the vision of himself insulted by Agamemnon, and the battering of Odysseus is nothing compared to the shock of Patroclus' death.

For each hero the return will be short-lived: Achilles returns strictly on the condition of his death, and Odysseus comes back to Ithaca only to have to leave again. But Troy will be taken and Ithaca preserved, because whatever their final fates, both heroes did return. Achilles' return is like a shot, Odysseus' the prepared progress of a master technician, but the fact of their return connects the two not only with each other but with the timeless patterns by which man has sought to understand and reaffirm the life he finds so precarious, so precious.

◄§ APPENDIX I §►

CHRONOLOGY

All dates are B.C.; *those before the sixth century are tentative and approximate.*

2000   Shortly before or after this date people who speak Greek appear in mainland Greece.

1600-   Minoan civilization flourishes on the island of Crete.
1400

1400   Sir Arthur Evans' date for the fall of Knossus; subsequent eclipse of Minoan power.

1400-   Great age of Mycenaean civilization in Greece.
1200

1200   Beginning of Dorian invasion.

1184   Eratosthenes' date for the Fall of Troy.

1150   Destruction of Mycenae; beginning of Greek "Dark Ages," to last until "Renaissance" of eighth and seventh centuries.

1000   End of Bronze Age; beginning of migrations to Asia Minor.

800-   Greek colonization throughout Mediterranean world.
550

750   Introduction of alphabet into Greece; Homeric poems written down.

650-   Age of Tyrants: rise of the city-state (*polis*).
500

490   Persian invasion of Greece repelled at Marathon.

480   Greeks defeat Persians again at naval battle of Salamis.

480-   Classical Age: Aeschylus (525-456), Sophocles (495-406), Euripides (480-406), Aristophanes (448-380), Pericles (500-429), Socrates (469-399), Plato (427-348), Aristotle (384-322).
400

431-   Peloponnesian War, ending in Sparta's defeat of Athens.
404

360   Philip succeeds to throne of Macedonia; attempts to unify Greece.

356-   Alexander the Great; succeeds to throne of Macedonia in 336.
323

301	Battle of Ipsus; subsequent partition of Alexander's empire into Syria, Egypt, and Macedonia.
323-146	Hellenistic Age; Alexandrian scholars edit Homeric poems.
146	Corinth destroyed; Greece becomes a Roman protectorate, later a province.

TRANSLATION AND
TRANSLATIONS

In his "Wife of Bath's Tale" Chaucer tells of the knight who had to choose between a wife who was faithful but ugly and one who was "yong and fair" but faithless. As has often been remarked, this is the classic predicament of the translator with respect to the work he has come to love so much that he presumes to recast it in his own language. It is a tribute to the zeal—or the perversity—of translators that these dispiriting alternatives are not wholly inhibiting, and that in their despite translators continue to seek the perilous compromises, the small victories, and the interesting failures that characterize every translation. The prospect is even bleaker for the translator of Homer—and by one count there have been thirty or so who have published English translations of the *Odyssey* —because he can never settle for even the alternative (and consolation) of fidelity. In the presence of a civilization that is passed, a language that is dead, and a music that is lost, he can never know quite what he is to be faithful to. Compare the much less baffling task of the translator who works from a modern foreign language. The French translator knows how French sounds, and by steeping himself in French literature, life, and language he can acquire that special empathy for the original material that is basic to any attempt to render it in another tongue. No such comforting resources are available to the translator of Homeric poetry, no matter how enterprising he may be. Though he can read that Aeschylus claimed that he dined at Homer's banquet table, he can never know how Homer's verse tasted to Aeschylus. Or, more materially, how Homer's hexameters sounded to a Greek of the seventh century who heard them recited by a minstrel at some Ionian festival or to an Athenian of the fifth century hearing them at the great festival of the Panathenaca. Or, in terms of the poem itself, how it felt to be a Phaeacian and, as in *Odyssey* VIII, to sit in the great hall of the king's palace and hear the blind bard Demodocus accompanying himself on his lyre as he sang of the Quarrel of Odysseus and

Achilles. Furthermore, it is passages like this from the *Odyssey* that remind us of another crucial factor in the aesthetics of the heroic age: this was an oral culture, without silent reading, and hence without the special habits of mind entailed by literacy. For hundreds of years Homer's audience was made up of listeners, not readers. Heroic efforts have been made recently to study and preserve the remnants of oral tradition that have persisted into our own period (mostly in Yugoslavia), but their vast remove from the conditions of Homeric Greece suggests caution in establishing analogies. Scholars can show us how oral poems are composed; it is less easy to determine how, for Homer, anyway, they were received; and it is almost impossible to hope for a corresponding effect by writing and publishing an English translation.

There are also technical differences between Greek and English. Greek is a highly inflected language, English is not; Greek word order is loose, English is strict; Greek has three numbers, singular, plural, and dual, where English has but two; Greek verbs have three voices, active, passive, and middle (a voice, partly analogous to the reflexive, used to show the subject's interest in the action of the verb), four main moods, indicative, imperative, subjunctive, and optative, and a rich and varied use of infinitives and participles; the English verb system, with its many monosyllables and its array of auxiliaries, does not work in the same way; Greek has a number of fairly distinct dialects, one of which, the Ionic, is used by Homer; modern English is, by comparison, extraordinarily standardized. These differences in language also extend to differences in verse form. The special form used by Homer is the dactylic hexameter. In ancient literature this is preeminently the epic meter, and it is used by Vergil in his *Aeneid*. By its name, the dactylic hexameter has six feet, usually dactyls ($- \smile \smile$), except for the last foot, which has two syllables, either a dactyl without a final syllable ($- \smile$) or a spondee ($--$). The poet may also substitute spondees elsewhere in the line to give a slow or heavy movement to his line, though Homer uses spondees more sparingly than Vergil, averaging fewer than two a line. The English equivalent of the dactylic hexameter is less familiar in British and American verse, though most readers remember isolated hexameters, such as "How art thou fallen from heaven, O Lucifer, son of the morning" (Isaiah 14:12), or the opening lines of Longfellow's *Evangeline:* "This is the forest primeval. The murmuring pines and the hemlock." English poetry has not been rich or fortunate in dactylic hexameters; the disproportionately high incidence of unstressed syllables required by this verse does not favor the heavier movement of English, and the long hexameter line, repeated too often, engenders a singsong effect that is both monotonous and distracting. (The Cotterill translation below shows what can happen to a passage of the *Odyssey* set in English hexameters.)

But even if a gifted translator were somehow to overcome the seemingly inherent disadvantages of the English dactylic hexameters, he would still be very uncertain how well his version could match the cadences of the original. English verse is read, or at best recited, with the metrical stresses usually coinciding with the speech stresses. This kind of recitation, with heavy emphasis on the metrical stresses, is the way Homeric epic is sometimes recited today—usually in classrooms where students labor to separate the dactyls from the spondees and get the scansion straight. Whatever limited value this practice may have for pedagogy, it certainly does not render the sound (whatever it was) of Homeric Greek. Admittedly, the study of Greek sounds and Greek metrics is notoriously difficult— an area in which, according to one expert, everything that is not problematical is trivial. However, there have been sporadic attempts, notably by W. H. D. Rouse in England, to revive the tonic accent, the system of varying musical pitches indicated by the three Greek accent marks, the acute ('), the grave (`), and the circumflex (^). Rouse's work is now being extended by Professor W. B. Stanford in his 1966 Sather lectures at the University of California, and when they are published, along with recordings of Professor Stanford's readings, we shall certainly be closer to the sound of Homeric Greek.

The most famous description of Homeric poetry, and at the same time a prescription for all translators of the *Iliad* and *Odyssey,* is that of Matthew Arnold in his essays, "On Translating Homer." "Homer's characteristic qualities are rapidity of movement, plainness of words and style, simplicity and directness of ideas, and, above all, nobleness, the grand manner." Not all of these qualities are always on display in any given passage, but they are useful criteria for the aspiring translator. Below is a passage of the *Odyssey,* the Sirens' Song of Book XII (184-91), and examples of the attempts made to translate this song into English. It is difficult to find passages in the *Odyssey,* like the war scenes in the *Iliad,* that are representative of the poem as a whole. Yet these eight lines have not been chosen wholly at random; they do sum up one of the characteristic perils that Odysseus must endure, and to be effective they must communicate in their sound and sense the terrible beauty of their appeal. Accordingly, they should bring out the best in any translator; after all, this is the song so beautiful that no mortal man could resist its Faustian temptation, the appeal to knowledge so powerful that it has been compared to the serpent's temptation in Genesis 3:5.

"Δεῦρ' ἄγ ἰών, πολύαιν' 'Οδυσεῦ, μέγα κῦδος 'Αχαιῶν,
νῆα κατάστησον, ἵνα νωϊτέρην ὄπ' ἀκούσῃς.
οὐ γάρ πώ τις τῇδε παρήλασε νηῒ μελαίνῃ,
πρὶν γ' ἡμέων μελίγηρυν ἀπὸ στομάτων ὄπ' ἀκοῦσαι·
ἀλλ' ὅ γε πεμψάμενος νεῖται καὶ πλείονα εἰδώς.
ἴδμεν γάρ τοι πάνθ' ὅσ' ἐνὶ Τροίῃ εὐρείῃ
'Αργεῖοι Τρῶές τε θεῶν ἰότητι μόγησαν·
ἴδμεν δ' ὅσσα γένηται ἐπὶ χθονὶ πουλυβοτείρῃ."

"Deur' ag' ion, poluain' Oduseu, mega kudos Achaion,
nea katasteson, hona noiteren op' akouses.
ou gar po tis tede parelase nei melaine,
prin g' hemeon meligerun apo stomaton op akousai•
all' ho ge pempsamenos neitai kai pleiona eidos.
idmen gar toi panth' hos eni Troie eureie
Argeioi Troes te theon iotete mogesan•
idmen d'hossa genetai epi chthoni pouluboteire."

Come here, O much-praised Odysseus, great glory of the Achaeans. Land your ship so that you may hear our two voices. For never yet did anyone sail by here in his dark ship before hearing the honey-speeched voice from our mouths; but then he goes on having had his pleasure and knowing more. For we know all that the Argives and the Trojans labored in broad Troy by the will of the gods; and we know what things may happen on the much-nourishing earth.

This is a fairly literal, and fairly pedestrian, translation. It has the merit of saying more or less what the Greek says. It even tries to render the Greek epithets (much-praised, much-nourishing), but often as not these epithets, so characteristic of Homer's style, come off in English as awkward and grotesque compound adjectives. But behind its surface simplicities is a whole array of impossible choices. First, the sound. How to reproduce what one translator has described as the "crooning vowels" of the first line? Or the slower movement of the first two spondees of the third line that match the heavy finality (For never yet . . .") of the Sirens' pronouncement? Or the change half way through the line from spondees to dactyls and from hard consonant sounds to the liquid sounds (l, m, n, r) of the passing boat? This translator has simply ignored the sound, but the Ideal Translator cannot. Beyond the sound the Ideal Translator has still other more technical problems. If he wants to render the passage precisely, then he must make sure that the English adjective used for Odysseus' epithet in the first line is reserved for him exclusively, as *poluain'* is by Homer. He must also translate *kudos* in the first line by a special word, for in Greek it has an "epic" sound and does not appear in Attic prose. Then there is the question of *noiteren*. It is an adjective designating the Greek dual, and as such it clearly signals that there are two Sirens. All right, but in the rest of the passage Homer reverts to the plural number. (Homer is not precise in his use of the dual.) Fortunately, this dual-plural distinction does not exist in English; but how necessary is it for the Ideal Translator to indicate this duality? Next, what about the "dark ship"? The word for "dark" literally means "black," but sometimes Homer seems to intend "dark"; so which should be used here? Then in the sixth line there is a sinister ambiguity in the use of an aorist participle for "enjoy" and a perfect participle for "know": whoever succumbs to the Sirens will have his momentary enjoyment first and a subsequent kind of knowledge quite different from what the Sirens are promising. And what to do with the Greek verb *mogesan?* It suggests all the hardships the Trojan War involved, the pain, struggle, effort, endurance, but it cannot be rendered by one of these alone. And finally, *theon* in line 190. What happens to a translation (like T. E. Lawrence's) when this word is consistently capitalized? Or when it is translated as "Heaven" or as the singular "God"? And so it goes, problems compounding problems, every solution a compromise, every compromise a betrayal, every betrayal a loss. Exit Ideal Translator.

Here are some translations of the Sirens' Song, selected to represent different periods and fashions of Homeric translation. First, George Chapman (1559-1634), the Elizabethan dramatist whose *Odyssey* appeared in 1616. Chapman did his translations of the *Iliad* and the *Odyssey* in part "to make great Homer's misticke meaning plain," which meant that he freely expanded the originals and occasionally glossed his translations with moralizing comments. He interpreted Odysseus' success in the *Odyssey* as an allegory of man's overcoming his passions by gradually subordinating them to "the Minds inward, constant, and unconquered Empire"; hence he understood the sea over which Odysseus sailed as the angry waters of human life, and his goal as the "onely true naturall countrie of every worthy man, whose haven is heaven and the next life." The Sirens of course threaten Odysseus' salvation, and in one line Chapman explicitly—and un-Homerically—identifies them as the "divell."

> Come here, thou worthy of a world of praise,
> That dost so high the Grecian glory raise,

Ulysses! Stay thy ship, and that song hear
That none past ever but it bent his ear,
But left him ravish'd, and instructed more
By us, than any ever heard before.
For we know all things whatsoever were
In wide Troy labour'd; whatsoever there
The Grecians and the Trojans both sustain'd
By those high issues that the Gods ordain'd.
And whatsoever all the earth can show
T'inform a knowledge of desert, we know.

Here "ravish'd" is a fine word to describe the Sirens' spell, reminding one of Donne's use of the same word in the last line of his "Batter my heart, three personed God." But there is also the Christian coloring in "those high issues that the Gods ordain'd"; and the difficulties of Chapman's style are evident in the dependent clauses in lines 4 to 6 that leave the referent of "any" unclear (any man? any song?) and in the obscurity of the last line's "knowledge of desert."

It is wrong to speak of Alexander Pope's (1688-1744) *Odyssey* when citing the Sirens' Song, because Book XII was translated by William Broome, one of Pope's two collaborators. Pope supervised and corrected Broome's work, but it is impossible to judge to what extent, if at all, his hand is in these lines.

Oh stay, O pride of Greece! Ulysses stay!
Oh cease thy course, and listen to our lay!
Blest is the man ordain'd our voice to hear.
The song instructs the soul and charms the ear.
Approach! thy soul shall into raptures rise!
Approach! and learn new wisdom from the wise!
We know whate'er the kings of mighty name
Achieved at Ilion in the field of fame;
Whate'er beneath the sun's bright journey lies.
Oh stay, and learn new wisdom from the wise!

Augustan verse is in much higher repute today than in Matthew Arnold's time (he is particularly hard on Pope), but the *Odyssey* in heroic couplets still demands a special adjustment for a reader fresh from the original. The couplet's rhymes and end-stops, its ten-syllable line, and its built-in antitheses impose on Homer a structure and movement wholly different from the spaciousness and discursiveness of the Greek. Yet a set piece like the Sirens' Song, where the Sirens' direct address to Odysseus itself falls into couplets, can well be accommodated to the technical conventions of this verse form. It is true that in this version the Sirens' offer (their song "instructs the soul and charms the ear") sounds more like a neo-classical aesthetic than a demonic temptation, but otherwise the lines are direct and fluent, and one can imagine Homer approving, though he did not use, a phrase like "the sun's bright journey."

The Butcher and Lang translation of the *Odyssey* was over-whelmingly popular in the early part of this century, particularly after it was made part of the Modern Library.

> Hither, come hither, renowned Odysseus, great glory of the Achaeans, here stay thy barque, that thou mayest listen to the voice of us twain. For none hath ever driven by this way in his black ship, till he hath heard from our lips the voice sweet as the honeycomb, and hath had joy thereof and gone on his way the wiser. For lo! we know all things, all the travail that in wide Troy-land the Argives and Trojans bare by the gods' designs, yea, and we know all that shall hereafter be upon the fruitful earth.

This is the "King James" version of the *Odyssey,* Homer's verse pervaded (or invaded) by biblical cadences and echoes. One can find scriptural parallels for practically every word and phrase in this translation, and perhaps in some way these borrowed feathers add a new beauty to Homer's lines and these hallowed echoes lend the *Odyssey* an unexpected prestige. Certainly, one of the oldest clichés of Homeric study is that the *Iliad* and the *Odyssey* were the "bible" of the Greeks. The difficulty, however, is that this pseudo-biblical translation, meant to reinforce Homer, often works to distort it. In this passage, for instance, the reader who is sensitive to the biblical translators' constant use of the words "travail" and "bare" to describe childbirth cannot help but be distracted by their use here in so radically different a context.

The *Odyssey* in English hexameters is available in a translation by H. B. Cotterill, published in 1911.

Come to us, famous Odysseus, thou glory of all the Achaians,
Stay but a moment the vessel and list to the song that we sing thee!
Never hath earth-born man passed here in his black-hulled vessel
Ere he hath listened to music of voices as sweet as the honey.
Here doth he taste of delight and fuller of knowledge he fareth,
Since that we all things know—what befell on the plains of the Troad—
All that was sent by the will of the gods to the Trojans and Argives,
Yea and whatever shall hap on the earth, which nourisheth all things.

Here are evident the difficulties imposed by the English hexameter: the limited number of unaccented syllables in English in the combinations required by the dactyl and the consequent need to import otiose words like "the" in the fourth line and "that" in the sixth; and the task of creating spondees—that is, two consecutive syllables receiving equal stress. The only kind of single word that approximates a spondee in English is a compound word, and so Cotterill finds himself in the uncomfortable position of having to create compound adjectives ("earth-born," black-hulled") which are not in the original at the same time that he is not translating those that are.

The next two excerpts are by translators who reacted strongly against the archaisms and artificialities of the translators of their time and sought to recover the speed and directness of the *Odyssey* in vigorous prose translations. The first (1900) is by Samuel Butler (who believed, among other things, that the Odyssey "was entirely written by a very young woman, who . . . introduced herself into her work under the name of Nausicaa").

> "Come here," they sang, "renowned Odysseus, honor to the Achaean name, and listen to our two voices. No one ever sailed past us without staying to hear the enchanting sweetness of our song—and he who listens will go on his way not only charmed, but wiser, for we know all the ills that the gods laid upon the Argives and the Trojans before Troy, and can tell you everything that is going to happen over the whole world."

This is indeed a relief after the "yea's" and the "lo's" and the "hither's" and "hath's" of Butcher and Lang, though it is odd that Butler, who is careful to preserve the Homeric dual ("our two voices"), says nothing about Odysseus' landing his ship, and "the whole world" is a very flat and colorless equivalent for Homer's "much-nourishing earth." However, his choice of "charmed" and "enchanted," though without literal warrant in the original, does retain the macabre ambiguity of the disastrous delights the Sirens offer.

The next version is excerpted from a translation of the *Odyssey* published in 1937 by W. H. D. Rouse. This translation, which has had great distribution in this country as a paperback, was Rouse's attempt to turn "into plain English" what he calls "the best story ever written," and at its best it does have Arnold's rapidity, plainness, and directness. Here is how Rouse translates the Sirens' Song.

> Come this way, most admirable Odysseus, glory of the nation! Stay your ships, and listen to our voice! No man ever yet sailed past this place, without first listening to the voice which sounds from our lips sweet as honey! No, he has a great treat and goes home a wiser man.

For we know all that the Argives and Trojans endured on the plains before Troy by the will of Heaven; and we know all that shall come to pass on the face of mother earth!

This passage shows some of the defects of Rouse's virtues: a forced breathlessness, aided by a liberal use of exclamation marks; a fondness for Briticisms (here, "a great treat"; elsewhere "nanny" and "I say"); a certain triteness ("mother earth"); in general, a sacrifice of Arnold's nobility, or what we might call dignity, so that passages as different in tone as the Cyclops' speech to his ram and Odysseus' speeches to the Suitors come across to the reader with equal shrillness.

Another popular paperback, indeed one of the bestsellers of the twentieth century, has been E. V. Rieu's prose translation of the *Odyssey* in the Penguin series.

> "Draw near," they sang, "illustrious Odysseus, flower of Achaean chivalry, and bring your ship to rest so that you may hear our voices. No seaman ever sailed his black ship past this spot without listening to the sweet tones that flow from our lips, and none that listened has not been delighted and gone on a wiser man. For we know all that the Argives and Trojans suffered on the broad plain of Troy by the will of the gods, and we have foreknowledge of all that is going to happen on this fruitful earth."

A good translation, although "spot" is not a very graceful word, "suffered" is perhaps too passive a rendering of the active efforts of the Trojans and the Argives, and "flower of Achaean chivalry" sounds more knightly than Homeric.

The most recent translation of the *Odyssey* (1961) has been a fine verse rendering by the gifted American poet Robert Fitzgerald. Fitzgerald uses, generally, a shorter line than Homer's (and also prefers the Greek spelling—Circe is Kirkê), averaging five stresses to the line. But when he comes to the Sirens' Song, he suddenly abandons this line for a series of stanzas centered and italicized on the page.

> *This way, oh turn your bows,*
> *   Akhaia's glory,*
> *As all the world allows—*
> *   Moor and be merry.*
>
> *Sweet coupled airs we sing.*
> *   No lonely seafarer*
> *Holds clear of entering*
> *   Our green mirror.*

Pleased by each purling note
  Like honey twining
From her throat and my throat,
  Who lies a-pining?

Sea rovers here take joy
  Voyaging onward,
As from our song of Troy
  Greybeard and rower-boy
  Goeth more learnèd.

All feats on that great field
  In the long warfare,
Dark days the bright gods willed,
  Wounds you bore there,

Argos' old soldiery
  On Troy beach teeming,
Charmed out of time we see.
No life on earth can be
  His from our dreaming.

Fitzgerald's is certainly the most extravagant solution to the problem of translating this untranslatable passage, and this recasting of the Sirens' Song defies the kind of analysis possible with the other versions. Whether an operation as radical as this is justified by the results must be largely a matter of taste. Perhaps the only criticism possible is to repeat what Richard Bentley said about Pope's *Iliad:* "It was a pretty poem, but must not be called Homer."

Paperback Translations of the Odyssey

E. V. Rieu (Penguin Books)
Robert Fitzgerald (Anchor Books)
W. H. D. Rouse (Mentor Book)
Butcher and Lang (Modern Library College Editions)
Samuel Butler (Washington Square Press)

⊷§ APPENDIX III ༆⊷

FURTHER READING

The best book to read about the *Odyssey* is the *Iliad*. Richmond Lattimore's verse translation (Chicago 1951) is still the preferred version, though some will favor Robert Fitzgerald's freer rendering (Anchor-Doubleday 1974). Fortunately, there are excellent guides to both translations, for Lattimore by Malcolm M. Willcock, *A Companion to the Iliad* (Chicago and Macmillan 1976), for Fitzgerald by James C. Hogan, *A Guide to the Iliad* (Anchor-Doubleday 1979). Still valuable is E. T. Owen's modest and illuminating *Story of the Iliad* (1946; Michigan 1966, and repr. Chicago and Bristol 1989), and more recent readers have been well served by Martin Mueller's *The Iliad* (1984) in the Unwin Critical Library, Seth Schein's *The Mortal Hero: An Introduction to Homer's Iliad* (California 1984), M. S. Silk's *Homer, the Iliad* (1986) in Cambridge's "Landmarks of World Literature" series, and Mark Edwards's *Homer: Poet of the Iliad* (Johns Hopkins 1987).

On the *Odyssey* side, W. B. Stanford's two-volume Greek text, with introduction and notes, in the Macmillan Classical Series (1947; 2nd ed. 1981) that has been indispensable for a generation of Greek students will be succeeded by Oxford's *Commentary on Homer's Odyssey* (1988), a three-volume work that originally appeared in Italian and has enlisted the efforts of some of the world's best Homerists. For the Greekless the Homer industry obligingly continues to produce a full line of critical materials, and some of the most notable—older books by W. J. Woodhouse, D. L. Page, and W. B. Stanford, more recent by G. S. Kirk, Bernard Fenik, Dorothea Wender, and Jenny Strauss Clay—have been remarked here in the endnotes. A commentary that is keyed to the Lattimore translation is Peter Jones's lively and informative *Homer's Odyssey* (Bristol 1988). More discursive are three splendid little books by Jasper Griffin, *Homer* (1980) in Hill and Wang's "Past Masters" series, *Homer on Life and Death* (Oxford 1980), and *Homer: the Odyssey* (1987), also in Cambridge's "Landmarks" series, as well as John Finley's stylish *Homer's Odyssey* (Harvard 1978). Recommended, too, are the *Odyssey* portions of Cedric Whitman's

Homer and the Heroic Tradition (Harvard 1958), Charles Beye's *The Iliad, the Odyssey, and the Epic Tradition* (Anchor-Doubleday 1966), and W. A. Camps's *Introduction to Homer* (Oxford 1980). Concentrating on aspects of the *Odyssey* are Norman Austin's sensitive *Archery at the Dark of the Moon: Poetic Problems in Homer's Odyssey* (California 1975) and Agathe Thornton's *People and Themes in Homer's Odyssey* (Methuen 1970). There are also valuable collections of essays: Charles H. Taylor, Jr., ed., *Essays on the Odyssey* (Bloomington 1963); Conny Nelson, ed., *Homer's Odyssey: A Critical Handbook* (Wadsworth 1969); and Howard Clarke, ed., *Twentieth Century Interpretations of the Odyssey* (Prentice-Hall 1983). And for surveys of Homeric criticism since the Middle Ages, there are J. L. Myres's *Homer and His Critics* (Routledge and Kegan Paul 1968) and Howard Clarke's *Homer's Readers: A Historical Introduction to the Iliad and the Odyssey* (Delaware 1980).

Finally, there is a special brotherhood of scholars and sailors who set out "in the wake of Odysseus" to locate in and around the Mediterranean (and sometimes in remoter parts of the world) the places Odysseus visited during his wanderings. This is a perilous enterprise, and even in antiquity a geographer named Eratosthenes reportedly remarked that "You will be able to locate the wanderings of Odysseus when you find the cobbler who stitched up his bag of winds." Still, nothing daunted, a long array of amateur Homerists have sought to vindicate their faith in Homer's literal accuracy by showing that somewhere out there is indeed a land of the Phaeacians and an island once called Ogygia. They never fail to find what they are looking for (though they rarely agree with one another on their identifications), perhaps because Homer's descriptions are so generalized and the topography of the Mediterranean world is so rich in caves and coves and islands and cliffs that there are enough "identifications" available to embarrass a Schliemann. The most famous of these enthusiasts was the nineteenth-century British writer Samuel Butler, whose *Authoress of the Odyssey* (1897; Chicago 1967) claimed not only that the poem was written by a Sicilian girl, most certainly Nausicaa, but that most of Odysseus' travels took him around the island of Sicily. A more recent example has been translated from the French, Gilbert Pillot's *The Secret Code of the Odyssey* (Abelard-Schumann 1972), which puts Odysseus onto the Atlantic Ocean and makes of his wanderings an elaborate exercise in cryptography. Readers can find a skeptical review of the evidence by J. V. Luce in chapters 3 to 6 of *The Quest for Ulysses* (Praeger and Thames & Hudson 1974).

✎§ NOTES §✎

Introduction

¹ The English translation here and in almost all the following citations is that of
E. V. Rieu, available in Penguin Classics paperback. They are reprinted here with the
kind permission of their publisher. Other notable translations are in verse by Richmond
Lattimore (New York 1965), with a fine introduction, and in prose by Walter Shewring
(Oxford 1980), with an introduction by G. S. Kirk. A highly recommended book-by-
book commentary is by Peter Jones, *Homer's Odyssey: A Companion to the English
Translation of Richmond Lattimore* (Bristol 1988).

² Basic are Albert B. Lord, *The Singer of Tales* (Cambridge, Mass. 1960) and Parry's
publications, which have been collected and prefaced with an informative introduction
by his son Adam Parry, in *The Making of Homeric Verse* (Oxford 1971). There are
excellent surveys of oral composition by Mark W. Edwards in the "Characteristics of
Homeric Poetry" section of his *Homer: Poet of the Iliad* (Baltimore 1987), pp. 15–123; and
by Jasper Griffin in "The Making of the *Odyssey*" section of his *Homer: The Odyssey*
(Cambridge 1987), pp. 7–35.

³ Michael Ventris and John Chadwick, *Documents in Mycenaean Greek*, 2nd ed.
(Cambridge 1973). On the evidential value of Linear B documents for Mycenaean
history and Homeric epic, see Chadwick, *The Mycenaean World* (Cambridge 1976).

⁴ Emily Vermeule, *Greece in the Bronze Age*, 2nd ed. (Chicago 1972); J. T. Hooker,
Mycenaean Greece (London 1976); Oswyn Murray, *Early Greece* (Brighton 1980); Lord
William Taylour, *The Mycenaeans*, rev. ed. (London 1983).

⁵ See "Homer the pseudo-historian" in Chadwick, *op. cit.*, pp. 180–86; and
A. G. Geddes, "Who's Who in 'Homeric' Society?" 34 (1984), 17–36. More optimistic
about the connections between Homer and history is J. V. Luce, *Homer and the Heroic Age*
(New York 1975). On the historicity of the Trojan War, Michael Wood, *In Search of the
Trojan War* (London 1985), is engaging but not persuasive; more skeptical are the
authors of the essays in *The Trojan War*, ed. Lin Foxhall and John K. Davies (Bristol
1985). It is important to remember that the matrix of Homeric poetry is primarily myth,
not Greek history, and that heroic poems of fighting and wandering cannot always be
counted on to deliver adequate and reliable information regarding social customs,
political institutions, and the details of everyday life.

⁶ "Homer has been rejected as evidence, with a pang." Vermeule, *op. cit.*, p. xi.

Chapter 1

¹ L. A. Post, "The Moral Pattern in Homer", *Transactions of the American Philological
Association*, 70 (1939), pp. 159–61.

² W. S. Anderson, "Calypso and Elysium", in *Essays on the Odyssey*, ed. C. H. Taylor,
Jr. (Bloomington 1963); rpt. from *Classical Journal*, 54 (1958), 2–11. Odysseus' final

victory over the sea is marked perhaps by the simile at XXIII, 384–88 that compares the dead Suitors to fish caught from the ocean; and in the Underworld of Book XI Tiresias prophesies that he will succumb to a mild death "far from the sea".

³ C. H. Taylor, Jr., "The Obstacles to Odysseus' Return", in *Essays on the Odyssey,* p. 89; rpr. from *The Yale Review,* 50 (1961), 369–80. Taylor connects the menace of the sea with another danger periodically affecting Odysseus, sleep, as in the Aeolus and Cattle of the Sun episodes, seeing them both, along with Calypso's cave and Circe's swine, as symbols of the unconscious, the instinctual, the absorptive which Odysseus must overcome in his struggle to survive and to maintain his identity and individuality.

⁴ Martin Nilsson, *A History of Greek Religion,* trans. F. J. Fielden, 2nd ed. (Oxford 1949), p. 96.

⁵ G. Wilson Knight, *The Imperial Theme* (London 1931), p. 136.

⁶ L. A. Post, *From Homer to Menander* (Berkeley 1951), p. 15.

⁷ Cedric Whitman, *Homer and the Heroic Tradition* (Cambridge, Mass. 1958), pp. 305–306.

⁸ S. Bassett, "The Suitors of Penelope", *Transactions of the American Philological Association,* 49 (1918), pp. 46–47.

⁹ W. B. Stanford, "The Suitors and Their Associates", Introduction to his edition of the *Odyssey,* 2nd ed. (London 1958), II, lii–lv.

¹⁰ A. H. F. Thornton, "Why Do the Suitors Feast in the House of Odysseus?", *AUMLA,* 20 (1963), pp. 341–45.

¹¹ R. W. B. Lewis, "Vergil and Homer: The Double Theme", *Furioso,* 5 (1950), p. 48. For many modern readers, such as Taylor, *op. cit.,* the *Odyssey* is essentially a poem about man's struggle for identity. See p. 56 above.

¹² W. H. Auden, "The Traveller".

¹³ G. E. Dimock, Jr., "The Name of Odysseus", *Essays on the Odyssey,* p. 72; rpr. from *The Hudson Review,* 9 (1956), pp. 52–70.

¹⁴ Nilsson, *op. cit.,* p. 158.

¹⁵ E. Abrahamson, "The Adventures of Odysseus", *Classical Journal,* 51 (1956), p. 313.

Chapter 2

¹ Not completely. There is still a persuasive "Analyst" case to be made for the uneasy coexistence in the second half of the *Odyssey* of two versions of Odysseus' homecoming, one, that he revealed himself at once to Penelope and together they plotted to recover some of their lost property by soliciting gifts from the Suitors (XVIII, 274–303) and then to hold the contest of the bow, and the present version, that he did not reveal his identity to Penelope until after the Suitors' deaths. For a discussion and references, see Sheila Murnaghan, *Disguise and Recognition in the Odyssey* (Princeton 1987), pp. 130–39. Fundamental to the compositional "problems" of the poem in the light of oral theory is Bernard Fenik, *Studies in the Odyssey* (Wiesbaden 1974).

² S. Bassett, "The Proems of the *Iliad* and the *Odyssey*", *American Journal of Philology,* 44 (1923), p. 346.

³ Stanford sees Homer "suggesting a latent father-son antagonism", *The Ulysses Theme* (London 1954), p. 60. Certainly mythology abounds in examples of the feared son who

will depose his father; there is even the non-Homeric account of Telegonus, Circe's son by Odysseus, who slew his father.

4 Stanford notes this omission of Odysseus' name from Telemachus' speech. *Odyssey*, note to I, 61, p. 222.

5 W. Allen, Jr., "The Theme of the Suitors in the *Odyssey*", *Transactions of the American Philological Association*, 70 (1939), p. 112, citing G. Calhoun, "Télémaque et le Plan de l'Odyssée", *Revue des Études grecques*, 47 (1934), pp. 155–56.

6 E. Bethe, *Homer: Dichtung und Sage* (Leipzig 1929), II, 15.

7 F. Klingner, "Über die vier ersten Bücher der Odyssee", *Berichte über die Verhandlungen der Sächsischen Akademie der Wissenschaften zu Leipzig*, 96 (1944), p. 14; rpr. in *Studien zur Griechischen und Römischen Literatur* (Zurich 1964), pp. 39–79.

8 C. W. Eckert, "Initiatory Motifs in the Story of Telemachus", *Twentieth Century Interpretations of the Odyssey*, ed. H. Clarke (Englewood Cliffs 1983), p. 45; rpr. from *Classical Journal*, 59 (1963), pp. 49–57.

9 The remainder of this paragraph closely paraphrases Klingner, *Studien*, pp. 74–79.

10 J. A. Scott, "The Journey Made by Telemachus and Its Influence on the Action of the *Odyssey*", *Classical Journal*, 13 (1918), p. 424.

11 G. Germain, *Genèse de l'Odyssée* (Paris 1954), p. 485.

Chapter 3

1 Post, "Moral Pattern", p. 163.

2 S. Bassett, "Athena and the Adventures of Odysseus", *Classical Journal*, 13 (1918), p. 528. For a discussion of the Athena-Odysseus relationship and a conclusion that they are rivals, see Jenny Strauss Clay, *The Wrath of Athena: Gods and Men in the Odyssey* (Princeton 1983).

3 Germain, *op. cit.*, p. 668.

4 Stanford, *Ulysses Theme*, p. 126. For an extensive treatment of Homeric allegories, Robert Lamberton, *Homer the Theologian: Neoplatonist Allegorical Reading and the Growth of the Epic Tradition* (Berkeley 1986).

5 D. L. Page, *The Homeric Odyssey* (Oxford 1955), p. 71.

6 Stanford, *op. cit.*, p. 50.

7 C. P. Segal, "The Phaeacians and the Symbolism of Odysseus' Return", *Arion*, I, 4 (1962), pp. 22.

8 Stanford, *op. cit.*, p. 52.

9 Post, *From Homer to Menander*, p. 14.

10 J. A. Scott, "The Sources of the *Odyssey*", *Classical Journal*, 12 (1916), p. 124.

11 W. J. Woodhouse, *The Composition of Homer's Odyssey* (Oxford 1930), pp. 39–40. Reconciliation is a significant theme at the end of the *Odyssey* (as in the scene of those old antagonists, Agamemnon and Achilles, at XXIV, 15–97), though some readers find it imposed rather summarily on Odysseus and the Suitors' relatives in Book XXIV.

12 George Steiner, *Tolstoy or Dostoevsky* (New York 1959), p. 115.

13 "The Jacobean Shakespeare", in *Jacobean Theatre*, ed. J. R. Brown and B. Harris (New York 1960), p. 20.

14 Stanford, *op. cit.*, p. 93.

Chapter 4

[1] W. K. C. Guthrie, *The Greeks and Their Gods* (Boston 1955), p. 156, citing Plutarch, *Isis et Osiris* 35, 365a. See E. R. Dodds, ed., *Bacchae*, 2nd ed. (Oxford 1960), pp. xi–xii.

[2] Martin Nilsson, *The Mycenaean Origin of Greek Mythology* (Berkeley 1932), p. 172.

[3] "The Meaning of the Eleusinian Mysteries", in *The Mysteries*, trans. R. Manheim (New York 1955), p. 25. A standard text, with introduction and notes, is *The Homeric Hymn to Demeter*, ed. N. J. Richardson (Oxford 1974).

[4] Jane Harrison, *Prolegomena to the the Study of Greek Religion* (Cambridge 1903), p. 342.

[5] Otto, *op. cit.*, p. 16.

[6] *Ibid.*, p. 18.

[6a] On the multiple connections between *The Homeric Hymn to Demeter* and the Homeric epics, see M. L. Lord, "Withdrawal and Return: An Epic Story Pattern in the Homeric Poems", *Classical Journal*, 62 (1967), pp. 241–48; and Cora Sowa, *Traditional Themes and the Homeric Hymns* (Chicago 1984). There seems to be substantial consensus that the basic pattern of both epics is the "Return of the Hero", though there is considerable speculation about how this pattern and its associated motifs of death and rebirth, or of rape, journey, disguise, and revenge (among others) may have shaped or influenced the two narratives. See A. B. Lord, *op. cit.*, p. 187; Michael Nagler, "The 'Eternal Return' in the Plot Structure of *The Iliad*", pp. 131–66, in his *Tradition and Spontaneity: A Study in the Oral Art of Homer* (Berkeley 1974); W. R. Nethercut, "The Epic Journey of Achilles", *Ramus*, 5 (1976), pp. 1–17; Douglas Frame, *The Myth of Return in Early Greek Epic* (New Haven 1978); Edwards, *op. cit.*, pp. 61–66. On Odysseus as a "returning god", Emily Kearns, "The Return of Odysseus: A Homeric Theoxeny", *Classical Quarterly*, 32 (1982). pp. 2–8. For K. W. Gransden the similar pattern in both poems of absence, return, and retribution "forms an argument in favour of the traditional view of a common authorship". "Homer and the Epics", in *The Legacy of Greece*, ed. M. I. Finley (Oxford 1981), p. 87. Readers should be aware that pattern-hunting, however intriguing, does entail a certain abstraction from the poems' local realities and the poet's specific language.

[7] L. A. Stella, *Il poema d'Ulisse* (Florence 1955), p. 272.

[8] The connection of death and marriage has its origins in mythology and endures as a literary archetype. Sophocles' doomed heroine (*Antigone*, 891) goes to wed the god of death, her "tomb, a marriage chamber". Says Capulet (*Romeo and Juliet*, IV.5): "Death is my son-in-law, death is my heir;/My daughter he hath wedded".

[9] Stanford discusses the problem in his note *ad loc*. For a lucid discussion of the poem's subsequent action, see Dorothea Wender, *The Last Scenes of the Odyssey* (Leiden 1978).

[10] I owe this observation to J. H. Finley. The practical difficulty of maintaining a live olive trunk as one of four bed posts in an enclosed room underscores the symbolic quality of this episode. R. M. Newton sees Odysseus' action here foreshadowed in the Ares-Aphrodite story (VIII, 266–366) where another clever husband with an injured leg, Hephaestus, has also constructed an unusual bed in order to test his wife. "Odysseus and Hephaestus in the *Odyssey*", *Classical Journal*, 83 (1987), pp. 13–20.

[11] Nilsson, *History*, pp. 26–27.

[12] *Ibid.*, p. 132.

[13] Hugh Lloyd-Jones, *The Justice of Zeus* (Berkeley 1971), pp. 166–67.

[14] T. A. Sinclair, *A History of Greek Political Thought* (London 1952), p. 16.

[15] Guthrie, *op. cit.*, pp. 23-24.

Chapter 5

[1] Page, *op. cit.*, p. 159. W. A. Camps, "Similarities and Differences Between *Iliad* and *Odyssey*", in his *Introduction to Homer* (Oxford 1980), pp. 2-4. Others claim to find an elaborate system of referents between the two epics. "I favor the hypothesis that the *Odyssey* did in fact know the *Iliad*", Pietro Pucci, *Odysseus Polutropos: Intertextual Readings in the Odyssey and the Iliad* (Cornell 1987), p. 18.

[2] Introduction to *Joseph Andrews* (New York 1948), p. xv.

[3] For the story and references, Robert Graves, *The Greek Myths* (London 1955), II, 280. See Stanford, *op. cit.*, p. 35.

[4] T. H. Gaster, *Thespis* (New York 1950), pp. 6-7 and Chap. II, *passim*.

[5] "Logically the Trojans are no better than the suitors of the *Odyssey* or than Aegisthus. Paris had taken his host's wife and would have been glad to kill him", Post, "Moral Pattern", p. 180.

[6] M. I. Finley, *The World of Odysseus* (New York 1954), p. 126.

[7] S. Bassett, "The Structural Similarities of the *Iliad* and the *Odyssey* as Revealed in the Treatment of the Hero's Fate", *Classical Journal*, 14 (1919), p. 559.

ITEMS CURRENTLY ON LOAN TO:

ame   : Hughes, Michael William
)   : XXXXX29269
ite   : 14/07/2014   Time: 12:33

TLE/ITEM   DUE DATE

he World's Greatest Symph... 05 Aug 2014
02995347

ethoven Gold : The essen.. 05 Aug 2014
03706220

oxanne - Man of war   05 Aug 2014
1953728D

he Trojan war : a new his... 06 Aug 2014
141008/1

e Iliad   09 Aug 2014
02465187

History of the world   11 Aug 2014
15592924

e art of the Odyssey   11 Aug 2014
01787406

lease retain this receipt and return
items before the due date.

ANK YOU for using your local library

INDEX*

A

Achilles, 7, 8, 10, 15, 25, 27, 35, 42, 62, 63, 71, 72, 83, Chap. V *passim.*
Aeaea, 8, 58, 64
Aedon, 28
Aegisthus, 10, 11, 12, 16, 21, 55, 62
Aeneas, 56, 60
Aeolia, 8
Aeolus, 27, 48, 57
Aeschylus, 12, 83, 84
Agamemnon, 10, 11, 12, 15, 16, 17, 27, 32, 35, 37, 38, 42, 44, 47, 54, 55, 62, 71, 77, 83, 94, 95
Agamemnon motif, 10–12
Agamemnon, 12
Aithon, 74
Ajax, 25, 35, 37, 47, 62, 63, 90
Ajax (Locrian), 38, 46
Alcinous, 19, 25, 36, 46, 52, 56, 61, 65, 77
Allegory, 48
Alybas, 24
Amphimedon, 84
Amphinomus, 21
Analysts, 30, 34, 61, 64
Andromache, 71, 95
Antaeus, 78
Anticleia, 47, 60, 61, 90
Antilochus, 35, 44
Antinous, 15, 16, 17, 18, 19, 21, 22, 28, 32, 33, 72, 76, 91, 94
Aphrodite, 53, 55
Apollo, 11, 17, 53, 75, 76
Archetype, 60
Ares, 55, 81
Argo, 66, 91

* References to Homer and Odysseus are *passim.*

Ariadne, 70
Aristaeus, 69
Artemis, 28, 53
Athena, 10, 11, 12, 13, 14, 15, 16, 18, 20, 21, 23, 24, 25, 26, 28, 31, 32, 33, 34, 35, 36, 38, 39, 40, 42, 43, 44, 46, 47, 49, 50, 52, 65, 68, 73, 76, 77, 78, 79, 80, 81, 83, 84, 85, 88, 89, 91, 92, 93, 95
Athens, 69, 80
Atreus, 11
Auden, W. H., 23

B

Bacchae, 69
"Ballad of Ares and Aphrodite," 55
Bed symbolism, 78
Bildungsroman, 43
Boeotia, 62
Briseis, 71, 93, 95
Bronze Age, 21, 68, 71

C

Calypso, 8, 28, 29, 38, 45, 46, 48, 49, 50, 51, 52, 65, 78, 79
Cassandra, 11, 46
Castor, 70
Cattle of the Sun, 8, 15, 46, 48
Change and permanence, 23–26
Charybdis, 48, 58, 64
Cheiron, 87
Chryses, 71
Cicero, 29
Cicones, 8, 48, 56, 65
Circe, 6, 8, 28, 48, 49, 58, 59, 60, 64, 78
Clytemnestra, 10, 11, 12, 27, 55, 62
Conrad, Joseph, 39
Ctesippus, 92

117